Supervision
Questions and Answers for Counsellors and Therapists

Supervision

Questions and Answers for Counsellors and Therapists

By

Moira Walker BA, MSc, FBACP

and

Michael Jacobs MA, FBACP

both of Bournemouth University

Series Editor
Michael Jacobs

W
WHURR PUBLISHERS
LONDON AND PHILADELPHIA

© 2004 Whurr Publishers Ltd
First published 2004
by Whurr Publishers Ltd
19b Compton Terrace
London N1 2UN England and
325 Chestnut Street, Philadelphia PA 19106 USA

Reprinted 2004

British Library Cataloguing in Publication Data

A catalogue record for this book
is available from the British Library.

ISBN 1 86156 414 7

Typeset by Adrian McLaughlin, a@microguides.net

Contents

Contributors   ix
Preface   xi

Chapter 1   1

The supervisee: initial questions

1.1   What is supervision? Is it for me or my client?   1
1.2   How am I expected to use supervision?   5
1.3   What are the different models of supervision?   7
1.4   How much supervision should I have?   11
1.5   What should I be looking for in a supervisor?   13
1.6   What is a 'verbatim' and is it useful?   17
1.7   Is it important for me to have a supervisor who has the same   20
       theoretical base as that which informs my training?
1.8   Is it necessary to present all my counselling work in super-   22
       vision?
1.9   I have been informed that I am to be supervised by my line   24
       manager. Is that not contrary to the guidelines for good
       practice?
1.10   Should I tell my clients that I present them in supervision?   25
1.11   Is it useful to tape sessions and play tapes back in super-   26
       vision?
1.12   Have you any advice on how I might make notes for the   29
       work I take to supervision?

Chapter 2   **31**

The supervisee: further issues

2.1   I have just started to work in primary care, and I wonder   31
       whether I should change my supervisor, who has always
       been in independent practice and is, I think, not familiar
       with short-term contracts?

2.2   My newest client has said that she was abused as a child.   33
       Should I, in this case, and in others where special know-
       ledge is involved, seek additional supervision from someone
       with that type of experience and expertise?

2.3   Is it wise to change supervisors every two years, in order to   37
       broaden experience?

2.4   I feel uncomfortable sometimes when my supervisor is crit-   38
       ical of the client or tells me how I should tackle particular
       aspects of the work. Is this usual?

2.5   My supervisor keeps mentioning 'parallel process'. What is   40
       that?

2.6   I have worked for many years as a counsellor and am cur-   48
       rently cutting down on the number of people I see – is it
       therefore all right for me to cut down on the amount of
       supervision I am used to receiving?

2.7   A colleague and I think we might form a group for peer   49
       supervision. Is peer supervision adequate? What helps it to
       be effective?

2.8   I have been offered the alternative of group supervision,   54
       having been used to seeing my supervisor one to one. What
       are the advantages and disadvantages of that, and how does
       it affect the number of hours I need to be supervised each
       month?

2.9   I am not very happy with the supervision I am receiving, but   55
       when I try to raise this with my supervisor she tells me it is
       because I have issues with her as an authority figure and I
       should take it to my own therapy. I think it's because I don't
       find her very effective. How can I resolve this?

Chapter 3   **59**

The supervisor: initial questions

3.1   Is it useful to seek training to be a supervisor? Is there   59
       really that much that I need to learn?

3.2   I have been asked if I would like to supervise for a local vol-   63
       untary counselling centre, and this will be my first
       experience as a supervisor. The centre wants me to see
       someone whom I know to be really experienced. Wouldn't
       it be better for me to see someone with little experience?

3.3   I believe it is valuable to offer a contract to supervisees.   65
       What elements should I ensure are included in it?

3.4   Have you any advice on the best way of keeping track of the   69
       different clients my various supervisees present in super-
       vision?

3.5   Do I have a role as a teacher when I am a supervisor? Some   74
       of the inexperienced counsellors I supervise seem to need
       instruction as much as the opportunity to reflect on their
       work.

3.6   How might I monitor the effectiveness of my work as a   77
       supervisor?

3.7   How far am I responsible for the work of my supervisees?   80
       Suppose a complaint is made against one of them by a
       client: could I be held responsible too?

3.8   I have just been asked to be an external supervisor for a stu-   83
       dent on a training course. What might this involve, and
       what do I need to ensure is in place to undertake this task
       properly?

3.9   I have to present a report at the end of the year on super-   86
       visees from a particular course as part of their assessment.
       Surely, the fact they know this will make it much more diffi-
       cult for them to be really honest about their work with me,
       especially if they say or do something that is bad practice.

3.10   I work full time as a therapist and am building up a super-   91
       vision practice. I am very clear about how many clients I
       take on, but how might I decide how many supervisees?

3.11   What is the ideal size for group supervision?   92

3.12   How much supervision of my supervision work should I   93
       have? And is this really necessary? Who supervises the
       supervisors of supervision?

Chapter 4   **95**

The supervisor: further issues

4.1   I am very concerned about the practice of one of my super-   95
       visees. What is the best way of tackling this?

4.2   One of my supervisees is particularly distressed at present   98
        following the death of a relative. Should I stop her seeing
        clients?

4.3   I am not sure how much I should allow a supervisee to pres-   103
        ent personal issues in supervision. I have one who is no
        longer in therapy. Should I recommend that he returns to
        therapy?

4.4   I have been approached by a counsellor who works quite dif-   107
        ferently from me but who has said she has heard I am a
        good supervisor. Is it wise for me to take her on? And, if I
        do, should I hold back on presenting ideas from my own ori-
        entation?

4.5   One of my supervisees is moving away and wants to contin-   109
        ue with me through telephone supervision. Will that be
        adequate? And what additional dynamics do I need to be
        aware of?

4.6   I have never supervised pairs before, but the centre I help in   112
        needs to introduce this for counsellors who have had indi-
        vidual supervision for a while. Is it basically the same as
        one-to-one supervision?

4.7   Group supervision seems to me to be no more than indi-   117
        vidual supervision in a group: one person presents but just
        to more people than the supervisor. I sometimes feel it gets
        rather tedious. How can I make more use of the group set-
        ting?

4.8   How do gender, race and other such issues show themselves   124
        in supervision?

Resources   **129**

        Suggestions for further reading   129
        References   130

Index   135

Contributors

Michael Jacobs MA (Oxon) is Visiting Fellow at The Institute of Health and Community Studies, Bournemouth University and in independent practice in Swanage, Dorset, where he supervises counsellors, sees clients and continues to write and edit. His books on psychodynamic counselling and therapy are used as key texts on many training courses – notably *The Presenting Past* (Open University Press), *Psychodynamic Counselling in Action* (Sage) and *Still Small Voice* (SPCK). He is a Fellow of the British Association for Counselling and Psychotherapy, and a psychodynamic and integrative psychotherapist registered with UKCP.

Moira Walker BA, MSc is Reader in Social Work at Bournemouth University. She is a UKCP-registered psychodynamic and integrative psychotherapist and Fellow of the British Association for Counselling and Psychotherapy. She was previously Director of Counselling Courses at Birkbeck College, University of London, and was at Leicester University for many years. Her particular area of interest both in practice and in research and writing is adult survivors of childhood abuse. Her books include *Surviving Secrets* (Open University Press), *Hidden Selves* (Open University Press) and *Abuse: Questions and Answers for Counsellors and Therapists* (Whurr).

Preface

This book is the distillation of many years' experience of teaching and practising supervision. We believe that we may have taught the first training course in supervision for counsellors and psychotherapists in a British university when we started in 1990. We approached the first of what were to be many five-day residential courses (sometimes as many as four a year) knowing that we had not ourselves received any particular training in supervision, because we knew of none that was available to us. Remarkably, we developed a model and a structure of training which worked the first time, and which only needed minor amendments in the years that followed. We appeared to have hit upon the right formula right from the start.

That formula involved a large amount of participation from those attending our courses, both on the course itself and back at home in practice. Observation of practice started on the first day (with ourselves as the guinea-pigs under scrutiny) and continued throughout, with each participant on the part 1 course having to supervise another under observation, and in the second part having to present a taped session from her or his home practice for analysis by tutors and peers. We introduced novel ways of group supervision as well, some of which appear to have been adopted in different organizations since.

Although we did not neglect theory, what mattered most for us, and we believe for our students, was a combination of practical skills, relevant knowledge and cooperative ways of working and communicating. In addressing the questions in this book, we have followed the same approach, concentrating upon practice and citing theory when it seems most relevant. More is being written and published about supervision year on year – our course reading list grew from an initial two pages to ten pages at the last count. There are also now many more training courses. Some, in our opinion, place too little stress upon the observation and critical assessment of practice, which is of course time-consuming and therefore more costly to stage. But it is, we believe, the best way of learning and sharpening skills, as long as the practitioner's training as a counsellor or psychotherapist has been thorough, covering theory and practice. Supervision is an extension of therapy itself, but it certainly involves different emphases and particular dimensions. Therefore, while we are both through our own training as therapists psychodynamic going on integrative, we have tried in this book to address supervision issues in such a way as to enable practitioners of most orientations to develop their models of therapy into supervisory practice in creative and responsible ways.

We have addressed questions asked by supervisees, especially those starting out in their training as psychotherapists and counsellors, and we have addressed in separate chapters those asked by supervisors, whether new to that role or with long experience of it. We do, however, cross refer between questions and chapters deliberately because supervisors can learn from some of the answers addressed to supervisees and supervisees can extend their understanding of the process by reading those answers concerned with a supervisor's perspective. This model of mutual learning lies at the heart of supervision.

This book is published at the point where we are ceasing teaching the courses we developed, although no doubt we shall continue to communicate our ideas in other places. It seems important to share more widely some of the thinking that up to now has been confined to those participating in our residential courses, sometimes trickling down to their own settings. In the work we have done in this field we are conscious that the methods we have favoured have indeed taught us as much as they have taught our student colleagues. Indeed, there is no doubt that our students have contributed as much to this book as the other authorities we have cited in our references. It is therefore fitting that we should express here our thanks to them for joining with us in such a creative learning experience, which we hope through this medium may in part be shared by others.

Michael Jacobs
Moira Walker
Swanage, Dorset
March 2004

Chapter 1

The supervisee: initial questions

1.1 What is supervision? Is it for me or my client?

Supervision is a necessary prerequisite in the training and practice of counsellors and psychotherapists, and is distinct from supervision as it is known in some other professions where it can be more akin to line management. For that reason some therapists dislike the word 'supervision', which implies a hierarchical relationship, and prefer the term 'consultancy'; the British Association for Counselling and Psychotherapy's (BACP) 'Ethical Framework for Good Practice in Counselling and Psychotherapy' refers to 'consultative support' alongside 'supervision' (2002: 7). The distinction between 'supervision' or 'consultative support' and 'management' is made clear in Question 1.9 below.

The question as it is phrased here suggests this difference: counselling and psychotherapy supervision serves the interest of the practitioner and the client, whereas management supervision, while being concerned for the customer or the client, as well as for the employee, is more about ensuring the efficient running of an organization. Nevertheless, as we shall argue, the place of an organization may also feature in counselling and psychotherapy supervision, but mostly from the supervisee's and the client's perspective. Supervision, in the sense in which it is used by counsellors and psychotherapists, is increasingly being recognized (or re-recognized) as an important aspect of other caring professions, such as social work and nursing.

In the information sheet 'S2', the BACP defines it as:

> . . . a formal arrangement for counsellors to discuss their work regularly with someone who is experienced in counselling and supervision. The task is to work together to ensure and develop the efficacy of the counsellor/client relationship. The agenda will be the counselling work and feeling about that work, together with the supervisor's reactions, comments and confrontations. Thus supervision is a process to maintain adequate standards of counselling and a method of consultancy to widen the horizons of an experienced practitioner. (BACP, undated)

1

This book extends that rather formal definition and considers in more detail many of the points made briefly in the BACP information sheet, such as choosing a supervisor (Question 1.5) and different types of supervision (Questions 1.3, 2.7, 3.11, 4.5, 4.6 and 4.7); we examine the content of supervision and its purpose more closely here. We choose to define supervision in this way: it is the joint exploration (whether in a one-to-one, pair or group situation) of material presented by the supervisee. It involves recognition that each party in supervision has different types of knowledge and experience, so that the supervisee has greater knowledge of the client than the supervisor, even if the supervisor may have greater experience of therapy than the supervisee. It rests on the belief that, despite large areas where there is little knowledge, in the dialogue of supervision itself there is always the possibility of greater understanding.

Although there is an important element of supervision that concentrates upon the supervisee, this is to serve its principal objective – that is the supervisee's work with clients – partly to ensure that the counsellor is working responsibly and ethically, partly so that the counsellor can consider alternative ways of responding to the client's material and reflecting upon aspects of the work which are less obvious when face-to-face with the client, but which can become clearer in discussion with another or others. All this serves the interests of the client, although our definition of supervision stresses that while it may cast some light, and will suggest other possibilities for responding and understanding, it certainly does not have all the answers.

But, if clients are therefore central to supervision, it is also concerned with the welfare of the counsellor, who, supported through supervision, may then become a more useful therapist to the client. The practice of therapy is a demanding one for the therapist as well as the client and, while it may be more stressful for the individual client than it usually is for the therapist, there are inevitably stresses upon the thinking and the emotions of the therapist: for the less experienced counsellor this includes anxiety about getting it right and containing the client's feelings; for the more experienced supervisee it is also stressful seeing several clients a day, several days a week. As the BACP information sheet 'S2' (undated) describes it, counsellors 'may become over-involved, ignore some important point, become confused as to what is taking place within a particular client or have undermining doubts about their own usefulness'.

Supervision is also one part of every training for counselling or psychotherapy: opportunities arise from the presentation of the work with clients to enhance therapeutic skills and to link theory to practice. The most obvious link with management is where the supervisor also has the function of evaluating and assessing the trainee, often on behalf of an agency or a training course. (This aspect, which clearly influences the supervisory relationship, is addressed in Question 3.8.) In these different ways, supervision attends to the needs of counsellors and therapists as well as their clients, with the intention that where it concentrates attention upon the practitioner this will feed back into her or his work with clients.

Supervision is distinct from personal therapy. It is hoped that it is a therapeutic experience for the supervisee, but it would be inappropriate if it concentrated too much on the supervisee (see also Question 4.3). Nor indeed should it provide therapy by proxy to the client! These two aspects need further consideration, which can be done from looking at the question from another angle – that of the supervisor. Is the supervisor's main concern the supervisee or the client? Such a question is posed by Jones (1989), who himself refers to the potential conflict of interests raised by Langs (1979). Jones suggests that concentration upon the supervisee could threaten the atmosphere of safety, which is essential for supervision. (We do not think Jones is suggesting that supervisors are then more likely to *confront* their supervisees in the work than *support* them.) Nevertheless, if supervision is too much taken up with what the supervisee is experiencing – whether generally in the work, or specifically with a particular client or with circumstances in the supervisee's life (see Question 4.2) – the danger is that the client gets lost. Strong feelings in the supervisee, and indeed in the supervisor, may provide some clues as to what the client could be experiencing (see Question 2.5 on parallel process), but where the supervisee's feelings dominate a supervision session this can be an indication either of the need to examine the supervision relationship or for the supervisee to have further personal help outside of supervision.

On the other hand, if the client becomes the sole focus of supervision, there are other dangers, which again Jones (1989) observes. These include supervisors using the opportunity to demonstrate their expertise and knowledge (a temptation if they are not engaged in much practice themselves), a collusive pairing between supervisor and supervisee whereby the client is put under the microscope and dissected analytically (which serves theory more than practice) or supervisors conducting the therapy through the supervisee, who carries out instructions and purveys interpretations at one remove! Kadushin (1968) refers to this 'Casework à trois' and 'I did as you told me', emphasizing the supervisee as looking for instructions from the supervisor, although Kadushin might just as well have observed that this is a game that some supervisors can play as well – 'Do as I tell you' (see Question 3.9).

Jones (1989) arrives at the most obvious solution to the dilemma of whether supervision is for the therapist or the client when he argues that it is essentially about the relationship between the two – what Langs (1979) calls 'the bi-polar field' – 'in supervision the central focus is the therapeutic bi-polar field, including the person as a therapist, but not the therapist as a person' (Jones, 1989: 510). The phrase 'the person as a therapist but not the therapist as a person' sets out a useful distinction.

Looking at the question from that point of view, we may be able to clarify the position. Supervisees need to bring to supervision the content of the sessions, which includes not just what the client said or expressed through mannerisms, appearance, etc. but also what the therapist said, felt and experienced before and after the session, wherever possible relating what one said or felt to what the other has expressed either verbally or less obviously.

To complicate matters, we have already acknowledged above that there are other elements in supervision, that it may also serve the interests of an agency and/or a training course, and that it certainly serves the interests of the profession, often being held up as the monitoring process of ethical practice: 'all our counsellors are supervised'. But, if the supervisor is protecting the interests of the agency, the training course and the profession, the bi-polar approach is insufficient. Supervision can be equally concerned, when it becomes necessary, with the relationship between supervisees and their agency, their training course or their professional association. Issues that spring from working in an agency or being on a training course may also be raised, since supervision is rightly concerned with the development of the supervisee; pressures that impede that progress, issues that conflict with the interests of the client and (looking to the wider context of the profession) matters that might lead to complaint or censure should be considered valid topics for discussion in supervision.

We agree with Jones that supervision can achieve these different but linked objectives only when it is a safe place, where sufficient trust has been created and where honesty is paramount. It cannot protect the interests of client, therapist, agency, course or profession where the style of supervision is so critical that the supervisee can report only the acceptable, or where the supervisee is so fearful that he or she cannot speak openly about self, the client and the setting. Supervision in these circumstances does not protect the interests of the client, the counsellor or the wider public.

It is the supervisor's responsibility, of course, to intervene if either the therapist or the client begins to so dominate the picture that other aspects are neglected. The new supervisee should not have to trouble whether it is for her or him or for the client. As we respond to Question 1.2, a supervisor should clarify at the start of any contract what he or she expects. Nevertheless, discussion of this particular question, considering the essential bi-polar focus of supervision, may assist the presentation of the work, as well as influence perhaps the choice of supervisor.

* * *

1.2 How am I expected to use supervision?

Just as there are many models of supervision (see Question 1.3) as well as differing views on what it is for (see Question 1.1), it follows that there are variations in understanding how a supervisee is expected to use supervision. These aspects are clearly related, as how supervision is used depends on how its roles and functions are understood and practised by the supervisor and supervisee. For instance, supervision can be understood as a process that focuses entirely on the patient or client and their intrapsychic world and their presenting issues; the supervisee is therefore expected to provide information about assessment, diagnosis and presentation of issues pertaining to that client. Other models may focus on the supervisee (such as person-centred supervision, see Mearns and Thorne, 1988: 73, and 2000: 196–211), while another model may explore the interactions and relationship between the client and supervisee. If the supervisor views herself or himself as an expert in theory and technique, the use of supervision is strikingly different in style and content from a supervisor who sees the process as essentially collegial and egalitarian.

This question invites many others. Who decides how supervision is to be used? Is this discussed or imposed? How should case material be presented? Does the supervisee present all her or his work? How does the use of supervision change over time and with greater experience? Do less experienced counsellors and therapists need to use the process differently from those who have considerable experience? How can it be used creatively? Our answers to this and other questions tackle some of these issues.

Taking first the question of who decides how it is to be used, the most obvious participants in the decision are the supervisor and supervisee. However, for supervisors who are employed by agencies or by training courses, and supervisees who are within these settings, there is another aspect to this equation. Agencies may require that supervision is used in particular ways. For example, an agency may state that a new referral is taken to supervision before the supervisee sees the client and may want the supervisor to approve the suitability of that case for that counsellor. Training courses can ask supervisors to supervise all training cases regularly, whereas others may want to focus in depth on just one. So expectations of the use of the supervision can be imposed to a greater or lesser extent from outside of the supervisory dyad. In those instances, the supervisor and supervisee can negotiate the style of the supervision – how the material is presented and explored – but there is an external constraint on its scope and extent.

How to present case material can be particularly perplexing for beginners, whereas those who are experienced have generally developed a clear sense of what they need to present and how this can best be achieved. The uncertainty of the beginner about the purpose of supervision and how to use it can be considerable, and this is not always sufficiently recognized by supervisors. One method of using supervision is for supervisees to select a case and refer to their case notes, detailing the content of all the sessions since it was last presented. This can be time-consuming and can become somewhat stagnant. The supervisor then comments on the session or sessions, and discussion between the two may or may not follow. Supervisors who see themselves as the expert can be less open to dialogue and debate and more likely to respond unilaterally. Other methods include a much more concise introduction to the client by using a précis of material from previous sessions followed by a discussion of this material (see Question 1.12 on making notes), focusing in depth and in detail on a very small amount of material that is nevertheless dynamically complex and significant, or presenting an issue that is common across cases (for example, an ethical concern or a particular presentation such as anorexia or depression) and exploring it; or concentrating on the relationship between the counsellor and the client and the insights this provides into the client's other relationships; a further aspect of this is the exploration of parallel process, whereby the supervisory relationship itself reflects and informs the counselling relationship (see Question 2.5).

There is a significant difference between using supervision to focus on *content* (what has been said) and using it to focus on *process* (the meaning of what is said, how it can be understood and what the counselling relationship might signify about the client's external and internal worlds and relationships). The theoretical orientation of the work is also highly significant. In a psychodynamic model, supervision usually explores counter-transference, transference, defences and projections, with the relationship of the counsellor and client at its core. In a cognitive framework, there is a focus on the structure, techniques and goals of the work.

Supervision can utilize more creative techniques. Although these may be more obviously available to group supervision (see Question 4.7), some techniques can be used by a supervisory dyad or triad. Role-plays are a good example: the supervisee can play the client with the supervisor taking on the counsellor role, or the supervisor can become the client with the counsellor playing herself or himself, followed by reflecting on what has been learnt from that experience. Role-plays can set out to replicate what actually happened in a session or provide space to play with new ideas and interventions.

We have previously noted that more experienced counsellors and therapists are likely to be clear about how they wish to use supervision. Whereas beginners can often want their supervisor to know about all their cases, the more experienced often prefer to concentrate on fewer clients at greater depth, recognizing that working on one case often informs another. If too many cases are presented, quality can be lost to quantity, and there is an accompanying danger of the supervisory process turning into a checklist, which is nearer in style to a managerial exercise than to clinical experience. For beginners who are understandably concerned that their supervisor knows about all their cases, it is still possible to provide depth and ongoing exploration of some cases. Time can be divided so that in each session 10 or 15 minutes are put aside for a brief overview of other work. On the other hand, where counsellors present a very small number of cases, they need to consider if other clients who might also need attention are being forgotten. One solution is for a time to be negotiated at regular intervals in which the whole caseload can be reviewed.

What is crucial is that at the beginning of any new supervisory relationship the supervisor and supervisee explore carefully the purpose of the supervision and how it is going to be used. Supervisors need to be clear regarding their expectations but also to recognize that for inexperienced practitioners supervision may be either an entirely new concept or one that has a very different meaning to them based on their experience of other work settings. They may therefore need help to consider how best to use the time and how best to present their cases. Whatever the level of experience of the counsellor, careful negotiation, discussion and agreement are vital in the initial stages. Agreement to review supervision at intervals is also helpful, as is initial agreement to acknowledge wherever possible, and then work on, any difficulties that arise. However, reviews should not be one-sided: they are not just for the supervisor to comment on the supervisee but also an opportunity to explore openly the process from both sides, so that each can give feedback to the other.

* * *

1.3   What are the different models of supervision?

A model is a way of organizing and conceptualizing ideas, beliefs and theories into a coherent and systematic form. Therefore a supervision model is a conceptual framework that has an underlying theoretical base, is describable, predictable and repeatable, and helps in providing and delivering clinical supervision. Models of supervision describe supervision's functions and purposes, the roles of those operating within it, and identify and emphasize key aspects of it. It is not possible here to describe all the models, but we can provide an overview of some key models, and so demonstrate the range of thinking currently available.

Proctor (1987) developed a three-function model, the functions being restorative, formative and normative. The restorative function is aimed at supporting the counsellor and encouraging self-awareness and self-development, the formative at enabling the development of professional knowledge and skills and encouraging reflection on clinical practice and the normative at ensuring that accountability, professional standards and quality are part of the process. In this model, any of these functions can become the focus of the work, and there is an emphasis on the shared responsibility of supervisor and supervisee.

Within a psychodynamic/analytic tradition there are many different supervisory models. The patient-centred model, or classical model, originated with Freud. In this model the supervisor's authority stems from the assumption that he or she is a relatively uninvolved expert with knowledge of both theory and technique which transcends that of the student. Difficulties that are experienced by the supervisee, or in the supervised treatment, are formulated in terms of the patient's dynamics and the supervisee's technical limitations or counter-transference problems. In the case of the latter, the supervisor will likely recommend that the supervisee take the issue to her or his own treatment (Frawley et al., 2001: 30).

This approach tends to be particularly didactic, with the focus of discussion and exploration kept at a safe distance from the actual supervisory dyad. It demands a high degree of technical knowledge from the supervisor, but it has considerable limitations if there are difficulties within the supervisory relationship or if the work that is being supervised goes badly. Scope for exploration is limited to exploring the counter-transference or identifying the patient's pathology as the source of difficulty. A poor supervisor can hide behind such a model and is rarely under scrutiny. Within the psychoanalytic tradition, a quite different model focuses on the supervisory relationship itself, particularly parallel process (Searles, 1955). This is discussed further in the answer to Question 2.5.

Carl Rogers (1942) was one of the first to use recorded interviews and transcripts for supervision purposes. This is often a surprise to those who see these aspects as more obviously fitting a cognitive–behavioural model. Rogers also argues that there is no clear distinction between therapy and supervision, believing that the facilitated conditions of empathy, warmth and genuineness are at the core of both and essential to both. Central to person-centred supervision is a belief in the desire and motivation to grow and develop. The immediate process is explored, and there is little place for unconscious processes.

Cognitive and behavioural approaches to supervision may well incorporate the need to establish a trusting relationship with the supervisee, but they have distinct differences to other approaches described here. Such supervision is based on a therapy that consists of identifiable tasks, requiring a specific skill. It therefore assists in the process of developing skills that can be applied and refined. It includes skills analysis and assessment, setting goals for trainees to undertake with their clients, the construction and implementation of strategies to accomplish goals, and the evaluation of learning.

There is also a developmental approach to supervision, with many variations to it. Underlying this model is a belief that supervisors change, develop and grow during the ongoing process of supervision and that supervisors can facilitate this change. As with the developing child, supervisees move through stages of development that may demand a different supervisory input and environment. Therefore, as Worthington (1987) notes, the behaviour of the supervisor changes as supervisees become more experienced. The supervisory relationship also changes. This is reflected in the experience of many new supervisees who are clear that, as they start practising, they want more advice, more reassurance, more help to locate relevant reading and generally more support, while those who are more experienced, although still wanting support, prefer a relationship that is more equal, egalitarian and collegial.

Carroll (1996) describes an educational model of supervision. Figure 1.1 (Carroll, 1996: 7) illustrates the continuum of education foci, which he suggests are also applicable to supervision. In this way, different models may be incorporated within the continuum.

Totally didactic teaching	Totally self-directed learning
Supervisor-centred	Supervisee-centred
Authoritative	Collegial
Information/facts-based	Awareness-based
Deductive	Inductive

Figure 1.1 Carroll's educational model of supervision.

Bradley (1997: 47) refers to role of the supervisor as an 'aide to the therapist' in the battle of emotions, rather than taking over the therapy and being in charge at one remove. Mollon (1997: 28) advocates supervision as a 'space for thinking', a place where the supervisor and supervisee can dream together. Lidmila (1997: 40–45) describes an exploratory or partnership model, noting that some supervisors become like detectives seeking after the truth, inquisitors demanding answers to questions or librarians asking about everything that went on in the session.

However, Gilbert and Evans (2000: 21) suggest that, if the supervisor emphasizes the relationship in supervision at the cost of monitoring and evaluation, supervision can become overly comfortable and friendly instead of, as it should be, challenging and educational.

Other models may be eclectic or integrative. Norcross and Halgin (1997) describe the principles of integrative supervision. These include customizing supervision to supervisees, assessing their needs, establishing an explicit contract, blending different supervision methods together and operating from a coherent framework. This differs from an eclectic model, which can be broadly defined as taking different aspects from many models on different occasions, whereas an integrative approach takes from what is already there and creates something new and distinct. An integrative model attempts to match supervision to the supervisee – taking into account her or his developmental level, style of working and presenting and sense of self – and assesses each person's level of therapeutic skills.

Our own definition of a working model of supervision, developed over many years, is based on our experience of supervising many therapists and counsellors working in different settings with different skill levels and coming from a range of theoretical perspectives (see Questions 1.7 and 4.4). Other supervisors may choose to work in particular contexts and only to supervise those who hold similar theoretical views to their own. That is clearly a significant decision, but for those who like to work across different modalities and settings we consider that it is particularly important to consider and review actively with colleagues and supervisees the style, model and methods being used. The model of supervision needs to operate smoothly at many levels and in many settings.

Our model incorporates the following: rigour without rigidity; while having a secure base in a theoretical framework and recognizing that it informs the supervisor's thinking, not needing to impose it on anyone else or seeing it as a panacea; and clarity about what the supervisor finds useful, combined with a desire to share it with others, yet knowing it might not always be useful to them. In this way, supervisors draw on their experience and learn from it, but do not take over the sessions with their knowledge and experience. It is important to be open to different ways of understanding, recognizing that these are valuable, informative and helpful. This model also recognizes that the supervisor can gain and learn from a supervisee's different orientation and approach without necessarily agreeing with all of it.

Creating a supportive environment is vital to our own model, but this does not preclude being challenging, although without being threatening or persecutory. It is vital to be able to say firmly and clearly when aspects of the supervisee's work are acceptable. However, if the supervisee perceives challenge as punitive, this must be explored, as must any other difficulties that arise. This means acknowledging the real relationship that exists in the supervisory dyad as well as exploring the impact of transferential and counter-transferential aspects. Therefore, an ongoing part of supervision is checking with supervisees their experience of the process and reflecting upon one's own, being aware of that part of the process too. It also means believing in an egalitarian basis to the relationship, while acknowledging the different roles within it.

Our preferred model recognizes that the supervisee is a whole person, which sometimes means acknowledging and working with their own difficulties. While it is important to recognize and hold to the different therapeutic roles of therapy and supervision, we recognize that supervision – just like other relationships – can be therapeutic without becoming therapy. It can be caring and offer valuable support. However, we also believe in providing a firm and reliable container to the supervisory process, particularly where there are boundary issues in the therapeutic work being presented. It is neither contradictory nor necessarily problematic to create clear and appropriate boundaries and offer support to and recognize the whole person; on the contrary, these are complementary and essential elements of the process.

* * *

1.4   How much supervision should I have?

The number of hours a counsellor or therapist needs to be supervised depends upon a number of factors:

(a) the professional organization of which he or she is a member, and the person's status within it
(b) if training outside a professional organization, the number of hours required by the independent or university course
(c) following qualification or full membership of a professional association, the requirements of the profession and the needs of the practitioner

Training courses normally insist upon weekly supervision; our own view is that supervision probably provides the best learning of all the elements in training, and in our past experience we have insisted upon two hours a week for the trainee psychotherapists for the main part of the course, and one and a half hours a week for trainee counsellors.

If the practitioner, following training, wishes to be accredited and remain accredited by the BACP, criterion 2 for counsellor accreditation states that he or she 'has an agreed formal arrangement for counselling supervision, as understood by BACP, of a minimum of one and a half hours monthly . . . and a commitment to continue this for the period of the accreditation' (see also BACP, 1998). Other professional associations may have similar rules, although member organizations of the UK Council for Psychotherapy (UKCP), for instance, differ in how much supervision is required, or even whether it is compulsory. Psychoanalytically based associations often see supervision as essential before full membership, but afterwards as a matter of the professional judgement of the practitioner: he or she may continue to be supervised weekly or less frequently, or may use supervision or consultancy whenever he or she feels it is necessary. In other sections of UKCP (the Humanistic and Integrative Section, for example) supervision is much more *de rigueur*.

This leaves open the situation for a practitioner who, upon qualification, can assess her or his own needs, and, curiously, the BACP counsellor who is not accredited and does not seek accreditation, where the 'Ethical Framework' simply states that 'all counsellors, psychotherapists, supervisors and trainers are required to receive supervision/consultative support for their work in accordance with professional requirements' (2002: 6), but leaves the amount of supervision open.

Since supervision, in our opinion, is more than an option in training, we believe it is a continuing opportunity for professional development and, furthermore, provides the reflection of another or others, which helps the practitioner to identify obscure aspects of the work that otherwise might not be recognized – so some form of consultancy or supervision remains essential. We would expect a counsellor following the end of formal training, and working towards BACP accreditation, in the early stages to have more than the minimum laid down, and, where a counsellor, accredited or not, has a large caseload, it is preferable for that person to have more frequent supervision than the minimum laid down by BACP. While it is impossible to take every client to supervision (see Question 1.8), the more opportunities there are for refreshment when working continuously with clients, the more value this will be for the clients themselves.

Nevertheless, we also recognize that it is both impossible with a substantial caseload to discuss every client every week and that supervision cannot cover every eventuality. With experience, it may become less essential, although it can still promote learning and reflection upon practice and lend support in what otherwise can become quite an isolated working environment. It was never the intention that supervision should be a place where all the work is talked about every time – indeed, if a counsellor attempts to do that, the scant attention that can be paid to each client hardly merits the effort. Presenting the same client each time can have a spin-off on all the other client work, and presenting monthly can have a spin-off on each week in between. Where the practitioner is not only experienced but also has fewer clients (nearing retirement, for example, or when working as an experienced volunteer seeing two or three clients each week), supervision may be much less frequent, although always with the recognition that, if anything needs discussing, consultancy should quickly be sought. Where supervision has to be paid for by the practitioner, yet the therapist is only seeing the occasional client, it does not make financial sense to have frequent supervision. In these different circumstances, we think it is right that counsellors and therapists should assess for themselves what they need and when.

The question of the appropriate time balance between individual super-vision and group supervision, especially for those who have to calculate a set amount of time for supervision, is addressed in the second part of Question 2.8.

* * *

1.5   What should I be looking for in a supervisor?

This question presupposes that there is a choice – whereas in agencies, and on some training courses, the supervisor will be allocated to the counsellor or the student. Nevertheless, even when there is no choice, our response may help indicate whether or not the supervisee is getting the best value from supervision. Unfortunately, not all supervisors come up to the speci-fications that we describe here. And those who are starting out as supervisees for the first time do not always know what to expect or what they should be receiving.

It is axiomatic that it is essential to have a good working relationship with a supervisor, especially when there is often sensitive and challenging, and sometimes painful or difficult work under discussion. Feeling con-tained and understood by a supervisor helps the counsellor develop the confidence they themselves need in order to provide a secure framework for their clients; in a similar way Winnicott (1964: 114–115) describes the father in a family as holding the mother who holds her baby. When start-ing as a counsellor, knowing that there is someone with whom the work can be shared each week acts as an essential support, helping to alleviate some of the anxiety that the novice inevitably feels.

At the start of our training courses for supervisors, we ask the students, who have all at one time been novice supervisees and are still currently in supervision, to appraise what is helpful and what is less helpful in the supervisors with whom they have worked, and whether qualities they looked for in a supervisor are as desirable when they first started coun-selling as when they become more experienced counsellors and therapists. From these discussions, we have been able to identify the most significant aspects of helpful and unhelpful supervisors, although it has to be said that in respect of some of the qualities there is some disagreement. For exam-ple, while some supervisees find it helpful when supervisors share their own experience, others find it distracting.

What to look for in a supervisor when starting out as a counsellor

Because a new counsellor has little experience of what supervision is (see Questions 1.1 and 1.2), the first expectation of a supervisor is that he or she informs the supervisee about how he or she likes to use the supervision session and what the ground rules are. Some may like the same case presented every week; others may like to listen to tapes (see Question 1.11). Some want a full or partial verbatim (see Question 1.6). Some like to listen to the whole presentation before speaking; others prefer to engage with anything that calls for comment at the time. Some like to draw theory out of practice, others to work on honing counselling skills. It is therefore important to know what is expected, and what preparation is necessary, and what the supervisor wants to achieve. Then (whether or not there is any choice) a supervisee has some idea of the supervisor's style. This information may also be important when selecting a supervisor, particularly when the supervisee is more experienced.

Related to this, and clearly necessary if this type of information is not forthcoming, a supervisee needs to feel free to ask questions. Some of these may be about supervision itself, including those features outlined in the above paragraph, while other questions may include matters such as confidentiality. As supervision proceeds, other questions will certainly arise relating to handling particular issues or concerning definitions of technical terms. The supervisee may also want to ask how he or she is doing. A supervisor may not always know the answer, or may want to encourage supervisees to find their own, and the supervisor needs to be able to say 'I don't know', as well as share their knowledge and experience when it is needed. It may therefore be helpful to prepare some questions before the first meeting and to check out what sort of response (both in terms of information and in terms of attitude) comes from the supervisor. It takes time to build up trust in each other, but these early indications may well contribute to that trust.

Trust is vital. If there is to be real learning, the supervisor needs to be the sort of person with whom all aspects of the work, including mistakes, can be shared, without any fear of cutting criticism on the one hand or inability to work with difficult issues on the other. Supervisors need to be critical, but not in a persecutory manner. Honesty is as essential in supervision as it is in therapy itself, and, if it is impossible to admit mistakes, ignorance or an inability to understand what the supervisor means, this not only makes a supervisor's task harder but also diminishes the potentiality for learning. Supervisors also need to be able to own their own mistakes.

Supervision when starting counselling often includes an assessment of the supervisee (see Question 3.8), but a good supervisor does not conduct the final assessment at session one. As the period of supervision progresses, and assessment gets nearer, he or she should be able to tell supervisees where they need to sharpen their knowledge and skills, and help them in that task. Supervisors are teachers first, assessors second. If a supervisee fails, it could be said that the supervisor has failed too.

Similarly, a supervisor needs to be honest and not frightened to challenge. Supervisors who are warm and accepting, just keeping a friendly eye on their supervisees, may in the end be useless. A good supervisor knows where a supervisee's cutting edge is, and speaks therefore not just to the level of experience and expertise that the individual supervisee has achieved but helps that supervisee to develop. If supervision becomes routine – either an obligation to meet on a training course or to meet BACP requirements for accreditation – it will lead nowhere.

When starting, it is likely that the supervisor will be of the same orientation as the new supervisee. Supervisors, like therapists, need to have a clear core model upon which they will for the most part draw. But, since training courses often seek to promote some understanding of other models, it is helpful to have a supervisor who is willing to engage with aspects of other orientations and with different ways of understanding the client and the therapeutic relationship. Our enquiries suggest that this ability to include insights from the wider therapeutic world is even more important in the supervision of experienced counsellors. There are few absolutes in this work, although a few certainties often help at the start!

There is also a question of the balance in the supervisor of being a teacher and a therapist (see Question 3.5). To some extent, supervisors model their style of therapy so that supervisees learn from the way they are as well as from what they say. But supervision is not therapy, and new supervisees in particular might expect their supervisor to be more active and more disclosing than they would be in the role of therapist. The therapist's stance is different (whatever the orientation) from being a teacher, a trainer or a supervisor. It may be helpful for a supervisor to share not just what they would do but what they have done in particular circumstances, as long as (as we have suggested above) they can share their mistakes as well, and as long as they do not take over the session for their own self-glorification. Since the supervisor is a teacher as well as a therapist, can he or she actively manage the time so the most can be made of the session? This may involve interrupting and actively asking about particular aspects in a way that the supervisor might not when in the role of therapist. These are quite different skills from those required of a therapist (except perhaps in limited-session therapy).

Yet supervision should also be therapeutic, and there is a question around how much the supervisee can refer to her or his own issues, especially where a personal issue may have influenced a particular response or lack of response to a client. Some supervisors, especially when the supervisee is already in therapy as part of the training, too rapidly suggest that such issues should be taken back to therapy, rather than discussed in supervision. On the other hand, no supervisee wants their supervisor to dwell on such personal issues and turn the whole session into therapy. This question is also one that affects more experienced counsellors in supervision, and to which we return below.

Finally, is the supervisor efficient? Does he or she start and finish the sessions on time? Are external interruptions kept at bay? Are sessions regular and changes in day or time fully discussed? Does the supervisor remember information about the clients who have already been presented – and explain what records he or she keeps as an aide-memoire (see Question 3.4)? It is important that the supervisor is sufficiently in control of the supervision contract and the session, to provide the supervisee with a real sense of safety – that holding environment which we alluded to above. Supervisees, whether new or experienced, need to feel clear about time boundaries, their own and the supervisor's respective responsibility for the work, and secure personally, that they will be appreciated and looked after, helped to learn and so make the most of the supervisory relationship.

What to look for in a supervisor when the supervisee is experienced

Much of what we have suggested about the qualities of a supervisor for new counsellors applies to what an experienced counsellor will be looking for when choosing a supervisor. But what might be stressed is the essential collegiality of the supervisory relationship with more experienced supervisees, whereby two experienced therapists, one in the role of supervisor, can spark each other off in the way they work with the material and with each other. This also suggests the value of the element of creative play with the material and openness to intuitive hunches – given that more experienced supervisees are less likely to take what is said in supervision as something that must be taken back into the next session with the client! This level of supervision might also expect to pay more attention to parallel process (see Question 2.5) and, where the supervisor uses a psychodynamic model, to transference and counter-transference not only in the therapeutic relationship but also in the supervisory relationship.

It is perhaps with the experienced supervisee that the value of a supervisor who is open to other orientations is most obvious. Some therapists and counsellors may deliberately seek out a supervisor who uses a different core model, at least for a time, in order to learn more about the potential value of an alternative approach (see Question 4.4).

The more experienced counsellor and therapist is probably no longer in personal therapy, which raises in a slightly different way the ability to include personal issues in the supervision, where they are relevant to the work, without the supervisor mindlessly suggesting that the supervisee goes back into therapy. Yet the supervisor also needs to have sufficient conviction to be able to warn a supervisee, who may in other respects be someone of equal experience, where he or she is needing to take particular care not to undertake certain work, should personal circumstances make it precarious.

* * *

Many of the qualities we describe as being appropriate in a supervisor may appear to be rather obvious, but our experience of training people who have already had much supervision suggests that some supervisors fall far short of these norms. They are described as overly critical, not necessarily of the supervisee but of the client, rather than enabling the counsellor to explore the client's difficulties (see Question 2.4). Less helpful supervisors can be rivalrous, or de-skill their supervisees through being brilliant, narcissistic, out to impress or acting like a guru. They use jargon and assume a level of confidence and competence the supervisee does not have. They never show fallibility or vulnerability. They may be controlling or rigid, not trusting the supervisee, and they constantly tell the supervisee what to do. They may use their own therapeutic model inflexibly. They can be totally accepting and not challenging, or totally challenging and not accepting. And, in this selection from a long list of negatives, they may allow the supervision to become embroiled in group or organizational pathologies.

At whatever stage therapists are in their counselling career, they have a right to good supervision. If supervision is not working well, it is time first to review it and, if it does not change, to seek a different supervisor or, where assigned to a supervisor, to raise the issues with both the supervisor and those who arranged the supervision. Our own experience of training therapists and counsellors in supervision is that in some instances this has led to positive changes in their relationship with their own supervisors but sometimes to the termination of the relationship. The horror stories we have heard remind us how important supervisor training is (see Question 3.1). Good supervisors are prepared to learn not just from their supervisees' experience but also from training and the monitoring of their supervision work, thus enabling all parties concerned to take a fresh look at what each is contributing to their work together.

* * *

1.6   What is a 'verbatim' and is it useful?

A verbatim is a word-for-word account of a session that replicates, as accurately and in as much detail as possible, everything that was said by both the client and the counsellor in the order in which it occurred. Generally, it is a written account and needs to be written immediately after the session, or very soon afterwards, in order to record as much as can be remembered. If supervision takes place immediately after a session, it is also interesting to attempt a verbal verbatim.

For counsellors who tape-record their work (see Question 1.11), it is a useful exercise to compare their verbatim recording with an actual recording. Having attempted this ourselves, and worked with others who have tried this, it is a salutary experience to be faced with how little can be recalled and how much is forgotten. When undertaking this type of comparison, it is potentially enlightening to explore what has been forgotten, distorted or altered. It invites an exploration of those aspects that have been mislaid or reframed and what this might indicate in process terms, so the recall of content moves to an exploration of process and meaning. However, it could be argued that tape-recording in itself means that counsellors do not concentrate in the same way, replacing their memory with a recording.

In terms of its usefulness, our impression is that this is a technique that is used far less nowadays. Those who are trained to write a verbatim know it to be very time-consuming (so it is not possible to undertake it routinely with a full caseload) but that it is a good exercise for encouraging accurate recall, training the memory and focusing on detail. Much depends on how the verbatim is used. We have known it used in supervision where the counsellor recounts the verbatim, the supervisor listens and then pronounces on it, rather like a traditional Oxbridge tutorial, where the student reads the essay, the tutor comments, the student notes down the pearls of wisdom and departs. It is a very traditional and, some would say, old-fashioned method of both teaching and supervision. There is little dialogue and little discussion. It can be a sterile and uninspiring process.

Underlying this question is another interesting one that might ask how far the supervisor can know what really goes on in a psychotherapy or counselling session and whether he or she needs to know in order to supervise effectively or, conversely, whether such detailed knowledge can be counter-productive. This clearly poses a major issue, which cannot be properly addressed here, about the nature of knowledge. What is important is to recognize that whether or not it is helpful to attempt to record accurately or recall a session in any detail is open to dispute and disagreement. For example, Arlow (1963: 588) argues against using verbatims or recordings, proposing that working with an unconsciously edited version of the session is advantageous:

> This view is in opposition to certain suggestions advanced concerning taping interviews or utilizing verbatim transcripts. The argument given in support of the complete transcript states that we know very little about what actually takes place during therapeutic sessions if we depend upon the incomplete record presented by the student. The supervisory situation, however, is so

structured as to invite a dynamic account of the interaction between the therapist and the patient. The supervisory situation discourages the courtroom type of transcript. This type of reporting resembles the voluminously detailed reports of anxious students. Such reports tend to discourage alertness on the part of the supervisor and are usually motivated by the defensive needs of the therapist.

However, it can also be argued that this does not have to be the case and that a verbatim can be used more creatively and helpfully. The verbatim can be written in such a way that not only are the words of the client and the responses of the counsellor recorded in two separate columns, but there is also a third column which provides space for the counsellor to consider and add process issues and retrospectively to suggest alternative responses. Counsellors can note what they were thinking and feeling at different points in the session. Why did they make that particular response? What were they feeling at the time? Was it helpful or unhelpful? Did it open up exploration or close it down? Were they saying too much or not enough? Would it have been better to keep quiet at that point? Did they miss anything of significance? Are there points at which they recognize lapses of memory? Are there parts they can remember only later in discussion with the supervisor and, if so, how do they understand this memory lapse? What might it be telling them? Were there times when they felt stuck? What questions and issues are raised that they wish to bring to supervision? Many such aspects can be noted and included in the verbatim so that, when these reflections are shared in the supervisory process, it enables a more lively debate and exploration. This aspect to writing up the session also encourages the practitioner to be thoughtful, self-reflective and self-challenging.

In the same way that tape-recordings can be used to explore in detail a segment of a session, a verbatim can be used. Just as exploring one case has significance for others, so examining in depth a few minutes of a session can be very illuminating and informative in respect of the whole session. It is fascinating how encouraging a supervisee to stay with a brief, and sometimes apparently insignificant, interchange can facilitate considerable insight. This can be particularly helpful for new counsellors at an early stage of training, since it assists them to recognize how sometimes a small detail or seemingly throw-away sentences hold enormous meaning. It can also help them to learn how to use supervision and make the most use of it.

The verbatim used in this way can encourage accurate listening and self-reflection, and can assist with noting and understanding detail and with training memory. Used badly it can be a sterile exercise devoid of any liveliness, which can repress creativity and become an excuse for the supervisor not to engage fully in the process.

* * *

1.7   Is it important for me to have a supervisor who has the same theoretical base as that which informs my training?

It is not clear from the question at what stage this counsellor is in her or his own training, although it is extremely significant to the response. Generally, if a counsellor or therapist is still in training, it is likely to be more helpful to have a supervisor who shares that background than one who does not. At this early stage the new practitioner is still trying to learn about, make sense of and develop their skills in one particular model. Moreover, he or she will be assessed on the basis of their competence in that model, and often a supervisor's reports are key to this process.

In this case, a supervisor who comes from a different theoretical base may confuse rather than clarify and may also increase the anxiety levels of the trainee, neither of which is conducive to effective learning or practice. During training, it is important that trainees are contained within a pre-dictable and consistent frame that allows them to develop their skills within it. To attempt to incorporate another base into their thinking and practice at any time before their core model has been well understood and incorporated is to unhelpfully complicate a process that already carries its own stresses. Additionally, supervisors who have taken the same or a similar training route themselves are far more likely to understand its requirements and so adjust their supervisory style and input accordingly.

There can be occasions when finding such a match is not possible. This is particularly likely to occur where the training takes place at some distance from where the trainee lives and practises, and where the supervision is not inhouse at the training centre but takes place in the trainee's locality. Those living in rural areas may especially struggle to find a supervisor who closely matches the orientation of their course. In this event, the best option is to find a skilled supervisor who, although having a different core model, is sympathetic to the training, is open and flexible, and will monitor with their supervisee the effectiveness of the supervision as it proceeds. It is important that such a supervisor understands what is required of them by the course, and it is the responsibility of the course and of the student to ensure that the supervisor has the necessary information. However, training courses need to remember that their students cannot communicate their needs clearly to supervisors if courses are not themselves transparent about their requirements. We have known courses that move the goal posts several times as the training progresses or which are not clear themselves where the goal posts actually are. This makes it an impossible task for supervisors who are outside that orientation, to say nothing of the struggling trainee who is likely to feel increasingly anxious, misused and powerless.

For those who are very newly qualified, the same restriction on choice of supervisor is likely to apply. At the stage of consolidating knowledge, as well as practising with less anxiety about assessment but without the containment of the training course, this is perhaps best done with a supervisor who thinks similarly. It is quite hard and not very helpful to be challenged by new ways of thinking and practising before the foundations of what has only recently been learnt are solid and sound. It is much easier to move on to new territory from a firm base. There is, of course, a developmental aspect to this. Consolidation of knowledge often leads to a process of thinking for oneself and to challenging established ideas. The strengths and weaknesses of the approach that has been taught begin to emerge, and as practitioners become more confident they are more able to explore other ways of thinking and intervening. Those who have been trained rather more purely in one approach often begin to move more towards a position of integration and become less model led as they become more experienced and confident. Even those who have trained in an integrative approach, where the theoretical base is drawn from more than one model, begin to understand what their own model of integration means.

It is at this point that many therapists and counsellors may consider it useful and appropriate to work with a supervisor who has a different theoretical orientation, especially where the supervisor is particularly skilled. In our experience, this can work extremely well and the supervisee can find new challenges and ideas exciting and thought-provoking, rather than anxiety-making. However, it should also be noted that this is not universal: some therapists choose never to move outside of their own theoretical persuasion, as they are entirely persuaded by it and do not want to move beyond it.

Some counsellors and therapists do not have a choice after they have qualified: they may be working in agencies which select a supervisor for them. There is a considerable difference between the counsellor who decides that it would be helpful and interesting to have a supervisor from another theoretical base, and consequently makes an informed and positive choice, and the counsellor who simply has one thrust upon them. In the latter case, both parties should explore the question of difference as fully as possible as this can be a real barrier to the effective use of supervision. It too easily invites a defensive position to be adopted by either or both participants. This can be actively or passively displayed – the latter is sometimes reflected in the supervisee who goes to supervision as required, but makes no use of it, or in a supervisor who solidly adheres to their own approach, denying evidence that it is clearly not working for the supervisee. A supervisor from a different theoretical base, chosen as such, can provide an extremely rich and valuable supervisory experience for a supervisee but, if enforced or entered into too early in the process of learning, this supervision can hinder rather than facilitate.

* * *

1.8   Is it necessary to present all my counselling work in supervision?

Since the questioner here is assumed to be starting out as a counsellor or therapist, we assume that he or she will in the initial stages of the training only be seeing two or three clients, in which case we recommend that all these clients are taken to supervision in rotation, either being presented each time or over two or three supervision sessions. Supervision is most effective, however, when it can concentrate upon one or two clients in more detail, rather than every client being reported and ticked off on a checklist. So in a particular session a supervisee might wish to report briefly on how the work with some clients is faring but spend most of the allocated time on one of them. In group supervision, concentration upon one client is also likely to be most useful for the group as well as the supervisee.

Managing the presentation of clients in this way, a supervisee can always prioritize a particular client where there is greater concern or more difficulty, without neglecting those who appear to be working more smoothly. But one of the advantages of supervision is that even the most apparently straightforward work has new light thrown upon it when it is talked about, making for even more effective work and for increased learning. It is also possible to deceive oneself that a particular piece of work is going well, only to find when presenting it that much has gone unnoticed. Similarly, if work is not going well, a supervisee might be tempted to present a client where he or she feels more confident, in order to please the supervisor. While therefore concentrating upon one or two clients, it is also important to ensure that every client is talked about at some time so that the sweet and the sour, the rewarding and the difficult, do not escape attention.

There is much to be said for presenting the same client session by session, at least for part of the time. Supervision is not just about picking up the pieces when things go wrong, or giving advice on how to handle tricky situations; it is also about tracing the course of a piece of work, from beginning through to its end, even when it appears to be progressing satisfactorily throughout. Supervisees sometimes think, for example, that as they approach the end of a contract with a client, having had some success in promoting change, they can move on to a different client, whom they are just starting to see or who is presenting more difficulty.

But this can neglect the importance of working well on endings: counsellors need to learn about all the different stages of therapy.

As the supervisee becomes more confident and more experienced, he or she may well take on more clients, or if employed in an agency could be seeing 20–30 clients a week – a heavy workload in our opinion, but one which nevertheless has to be sustained in several situations. Then it is impossible to refer to all the clients in any session without trivializing the supervision time, and it would probably be counter-productive even to take them in rotation to supervision. While supervision in its early stages serves the interests of basic training as well as ensuring the safety of the client and the counsellor, with more experienced supervisees it ceases to need to function in such a clear guardianship manner. Supervisees are trusted to distinguish themselves when a particular client or a particular session needs to be presented, and to leave to one side those who are progressing without apparent difficulty. Experienced counsellors may still wish to concentrate their time upon one client, since in the minutiae of the interaction much will continue to be learned that can be applied to the work with other clients, both currently and in the future.

Nevertheless, it remains important, especially for those with heavy caseloads, that a supervisor has an overall perspective of the work. Therefore, from time to time, part of a session may be usefully devoted to looking at the number of clients, what stages they are at in their contracts, at whether or not the counsellor is carrying too many distressing cases and therefore needs to be careful not to take on any more for the time being (working with survivors of abuse, for example), and at whether there are features arising from the work overall that merit particular attention in the therapist's continuing professional development.

What needs to be borne in mind throughout, in both supervisee and supervisor, is that however rational the choice is, of how many and who is to be presented in supervision, it is not until the client is actually talked about that both parties can really see whether the work with that client needs more attention. It probably always does, since, however experienced the therapist, there is always more that emerges from talking about it at one remove. As we have written in the answer to Question 1.1, 'in the dialogue of supervision itself there is always the possibility of greater understanding' (p. 2). For that reason, while we can confidently suggest that it is unnecessary for the counsellor who is gaining in skill and confidence to present every client in supervision, no therapist can ever be sure that work with a particular client would not benefit from being discussed with the 'outsider' in the therapeutic relationship, the supervisor.

* * *

1.9   I have been informed that I am to be supervised by my line manager. Is that not contrary to the guidelines for good practice?

Supervision for counsellors and therapists is frequently misunderstood by those who hold the purse strings in organizations, and sometimes by managers to whom counsellors are responsible. Thinking that supervision means reviewing caseloads, checking statistics, increasing efficiency, they assume that the line manager can provide it, as he or she does for other employees.

The 'Ethical Framework' (BACP, 2002: 7) makes it clear that there is a general obligation upon BACP members 'to receive supervision/consultative support independently of any managerial relationships'. The arguments for this should be clear: apart from a manager not necessarily possessing any knowledge of counselling, and therefore unable to supervise the work clinically (even though the manager may supervise the work organizationally), even where a manager is also a counsellor, there can be a conflict of interest between the two roles, for example the head of a counselling service wanting to see more throughput of clients in order to please funders may exert overt or covert pressure on a supervisee to finish working with clients earlier than an independent supervisor would. While it is important that supervisors, whether or not they are employed by or paid for by organizations, know something of the goals and pressures on the organization and the resultant dynamics for counsellors working in the organization, supervisors who are independent of management can make a rather more objective assessment of what is good for the client under discussion or how better to handle a situation where there is a conflict between the interests of the client and the interests of the organization employing the counsellor.

Nevertheless, we would not wish to condemn as unethical circumstances where the line manager is also the supervisor, for example in small services where there is no financial assistance for separate supervision or an insufficient number of therapists within the service to act as supervisors to others. What is important in these situations is that arrangements are made for the supervisee to have access to a third person who can act as a consultant or arbitrator should any difficulties with the service or the line manager arise that cannot be handled in house and from whom supervisees can ask for external assistance without prejudicing their position within the service. Here the twin terms used in the BACP's 'Ethical Framework' 'supervision/consultative support' suggest a way through such difficulties. Where a supervisee has to have supervision with a person who is also their line manager, providing that person is an experienced supervisor, consultative support should always be made available to them outside that supervisory relationship.

* * *

1.10 Should I tell my clients that I present them in supervision?

Openness about working practices is important at the start of every thera-peutic contract. It is necessary, for practical purposes, to ensure that potential clients know that a counsellor works to set hours and to a fixed time, what fees (if any) will be charged and what penalty there may be for cancelled or missed sessions. In addition, it is normally considered helpful for therapy that there is a clear agreement about its duration (whether short term with a fixed number of sessions or open-ended) and in some instances to ensure clarity about the goals of therapy. The question of telling clients about supervision is part of this general background infor-mation and discussion.

In other words, whether verbally or (perhaps more usefully) through printed notes, some details about the therapist's practice are important, with the amount of information provided being decided by the individual coun-sellor or agency. It might be expected, especially where it is a requirement for a counsellor or a therapist to have regular supervision, not least for contin-ued membership of their professional association, that a general reference to this will form part of such information, for example 'I am regularly super-vised upon my work' or 'Counsellors and psychotherapists are expected to have consultancy or supervision, and this means they may discuss some of their client work'. This alerts all clients to the fact that they may be talked about in supervision, although this is quite different from actually telling a particular client that he or she is taken to supervision, and different again from even referring to supervision in the session: 'I talked about this with my supervisor recently, and she felt . . .'. Such references might be extremely dis-turbing or distracting to a client, although we can think of some circumstances where it might be felt to be containing and reassuring.

Since the idea of being talked about with another person, and the impli-cations of that for confidentiality, may affect any client, it may therefore be wise to add a rider to the information about being supervised, such as 'If you have any anxieties about this, we can discuss it'. This leaves it with the client to raise the issue, unless it becomes clear from more oblique refer-ences that they have concerns about it, in which case it can again be raised in a less specific way: 'When you say you are worried about your line man-ager discussing you with personnel, are you perhaps saying that you also worry whether or not I talk about you outside the session?'

We suggest it is possible to be relaxed about providing such general information, since it confirms the safety net that supports a counsellor's work. We do not ourselves think that it is necessary to inform particular clients either that they are discussed or when they are discussed in super-vision. For most clients this would be to intrude upon what they wish to talk about in any particular session. What is more important is to know how to respond if a client asks directly, 'Do you talk about me in supervision?'. The most useful response to such a question is not to answer it at once but to explore with the client what lies behind the question: 'Why do you ask?' and perhaps adding 'What would concern you about that if I did?'. It may of course not be concern, just interest on the client's part, but such a question is more likely to indicate a worry of some kind: the client may be anxious about confidentiality, may (especially if in the therapy world) want to check that the supervisor does not know her or him in another role or may even have some anxiety about the counsellor's competence. It is the underlying reason for such a question that should be explored first. Such unpacking of the question may render any further answer unnecessary or, if it is clear that a definite answer needs to be given to the client, it can be framed in such a way as to address the particular concerns that the client has shared.

* * *

1.11 Is it useful to tape sessions and play tapes back in supervision?

There was a time when one of us had considerable reservations about the use of audiotapes of sessions with clients, not because of the value of listening to the tapes themselves but because of the effect recording might have on the therapist and the client (Jacobs, 1981). There was good reason for this, but also undue defensiveness. The good reason was because at the time a supervisee was wanting to record sessions because he could never recall anything of his sessions except the most sketchy information, which often included what he said, but not much of what the client expressed. The concern then was that the taping would not facilitate, as was necessary, this person's memory, which needed to be developed not just for reporting in supervision but in order to remember when working with a client what had been said. Nevertheless, there was also a defensive stance in the objection to taping, stemming from an over-preoccupation with what taping would do to the therapeutic relationship. This concern was partly alleviated through an awareness of the debate about taping becoming more positive in the literature (Aveline, 1992; Kachele et al., 1992; see also Jacobs, 1993: 5–9).

Since then it has become clear how valuable tapes can be, particularly when it comes to assessing the work of a counsellor and, indeed, of a supervisor. As Aveline writes: 'Recording provides direct, factually correct access to the therapy session which on that level cannot be matched by the common, indirect method in supervision of the supervisee giving a recollected and impressionist account of what happened' (1992: 347). Even if audio or video recording still alters the process, without it supervision is what Zinkin (1988: 24) calls a 'shared fantasy', where the therapist shares what he or she imagines the therapist and client have been doing together, and the supervisor tries to imagine it too. As a result, since we are aware of how easy it is for self-reports to idealize what happened, to forget what went wrong and to unintentionally describe only what might have been said, we have for many years required the presentation of tapes in the training of counsellors and psychotherapists as part of the final assessment, and we have stressed the importance of supervisors also taping supervision sessions not only for assessment but also for the rich learning that can come from working on the detail of the supervisor's interventions.

There remain, however, two important issues about taping. The first is that recording sessions certainly has an impact upon the process, although not as much as one of us once feared. While it is obvious that taping for supervision needs to be agreed with the client, this needs to be done with care. In the first instance, and as distinct from the answer we gave to Question 1.10, where we do not think it necessary to tell a specific client that he or she was being discussed in supervision, or for assessment purposes, asking for permission to tape clearly tells a client that he or she will be talked about. Some will not mind this at all, especially if they are encouraged by the emphasis on the importance of the therapist's professional development. Others may decline, and feel confident in doing so. But there may be some clients who agree because they believe this will please the therapist, of which more below, and others who, though they decline, will be concerned that they have frustrated the therapist. Therefore, when permission is granted, it is important to check that this is sincerely offered and to remind the client that at any time he or she may ask for the tape to be paused or removed altogether. Those who work from a psychodynamic perspective will also want to remain alert to oblique references to the tape recorder, even if it is not spoken of directly, and to explore with the client underlying feelings about its presence, about its being discussed elsewhere, about confidentiality and so on. One of us, recording a client to present in supervision, was very conscious to begin with of the need to listen out for clues to what the client might be feeling about being recorded, even though she had talked it through fully before agreeing to the exercise, but even then missed a reference in a particularly important taped session to others being present in an operating theatre – a reference, it seemed upon reflection, and with the help of a supervisor's observation, to the client's experiences being overheard by others (Jacobs, 1996a: 12, 112).

It is important to try to distinguish agreement from the client, which comes from a position of confidence, and agreement that comes from compliance. It is easy to imagine how a client who has been abused in childhood, having been told that it will be good for her, and will please the abuser, might over-readily comply with the therapist's request to record the session. One of us, in a variation upon this, was asked by the client who had been abused whether *she* could record the sessions: she needed to be sure that if anything went amiss she had evidence of this on tape.

Furthermore, if taping is acceptable, it should not be for a one-off or occasional session. The tape-recorder itself needs to be introduced at first without actually using it to record, so that adjustment can be made to its presence in the room. When taping starts the client needs to be told, and assured, as we have already referred to above, that if at any point he or she wants the tape turned off, or paused, it will be done without question. Taping should take place at every session, whether or not the tape is listened to afterwards, whether or not it is used in supervision (or submitted for assessment). In other words, it gradually becomes an integral part of the situation, so that, while it is not altogether forgotten, at least it ceases to be so intrusive. It is also worth considering whether, in the agreement to taping, the client might be encouraged to ask for a copy of any tape that he or she feels might be helpful to play outside the session: there is no reason why clients, as much as their therapists, should not be encouraged to use this way of reflecting on what was said.

Having recorded sessions, the question remains how to use the recordings in supervision. Playing a whole tape in one session is clearly an inefficient use of time: it leaves no room for the supervisor (or others who may be present) to comment. There are therefore two ways of using tapes, both of which depend upon listening to them before supervision. The first is to play one or more extracts of parts of the counselling session that particularly call for examination and comment, extracts that can be contextualized by describing what led up to them, and perhaps what followed them. Being able to listen to the tapes in supervision itself brings the work of the supervisee alive for the supervisor (and for other supervisees present). An alternative is to transcribe part or all of the tape before the supervision session and to present these transcripts to the supervisor (and any other supervisees) either before or during the session. Longer transcripts are obviously better read beforehand; shorter transcripts can be read at the time. Reading a transcript, even of five minutes of a session, is less time-consuming than listening to the same five minutes 'live', although playing a tape and following the transcript provide even greater clarity. Comments for later discussion can be jotted down on the transcript (always to be returned to the supervisee at the end of the session just as tapes must also be erased), and the pace and tone of the two participants on the tape enhances the detail of the words on paper.

Transcribing a whole session takes a long time, but so too does listening to it before supervision in order to identify parts to be played in and/or transcribed for the supervision session itself. Nevertheless, this preparation is itself a type of supervision, so that even at that point, as yet without the benefit of others' contributions to understanding, the counsellor hears and notices details that were not spotted during the therapy session itself. All this helps to develop the therapist's 'internal supervisor' (Casement, 1985).

This latter point illustrates another use of tapes: supervision in the presence of others is indisputably of the most value because it is the emotional distance of the other from the therapy itself that allows more dimensions to be seen and makes for the supervisor's 'potential usefulness' (Searles, 1962: 587), but self-reflection is also a vital part of a therapist's practice. If notes made following sessions (see Questions 1.6 and 1.12) are used for reflection, and tapes recorded during sessions are played back, this contributes greatly to the awareness and thinking of the counsellor, in addition to the formal supervisory session.

* * *

1.12 Have you any advice on how I might make notes for the work I take to supervision?

If a counsellor is just starting out in practice, as a trainee, it is likely that he or she will be seeing no more than two or three clients. As we advise in the answer to Question 1.8, it is going to be necessary to present each of these clients in turn in supervision, partly to ensure that the work is checked in supervision, whether or not it is going well, and partly because there will be much basic learning from presenting it all. But more experienced practitioners, especially those seeing a larger number of clients, may present only those who raise key issues or may present one client consistently in order to learn from working through the whole contract from beginning to end. Whether it is a trainee or an experienced counsellor we are considering, the notes made for supervision will probably need to be made in a similar way; the difference for experienced counsellors is that they may make shorter notes on those clients whom they do not normally present.

We distinguish, therefore, between notes that are made for the purpose of having a concise record of the work and those that are made when presenting a client in supervision. One method of recording concise notes, full enough to contain the most relevant information but brief enough to make in the times between sessions, is set out in the third chapter of *Psychodynamic Counselling in Action* (Jacobs, 2004). But when making notes before a supervision session, where a particular client or clients are to be presented, such notes probably need to be more extensive – unless the supervisee has a very good memory for the order and the detail of the interactions between client and counsellor. A supervisor wishes to know as much as possible. The more the supervisor knows, the more he or she will be able to reflect on it and make helpful suggestions. But, where clients are not regularly taken to supervision, shorter notes are normally all that is necessary. If a supervisee decides to present a client not normally taken to supervision, it is obviously possible to make a fuller record of the session in question.

We are already distinguishing in our answer here between the background information about a client on the one hand – the client's presenting problems, her or his known history, factual information about family of origin, present relationships, etc. – and the detail of the actual session or sessions with the therapist on the other. Background information can be recorded as one aspect of a set of notes and be kept at hand ready to answer any questions that may arise in supervision. In the answer to Question 3.4, we set out a method of recording that supervisors can use and which depends upon the supervisee providing some of that basic information and retaining it to be re-presented each time the client is talked about. We recommend that form of factual information to the supervisee as much as to the supervisor.

But supervision is most effective when, in addition to the basic information, the detail of the interaction in any one session or sessions can be reported. It is to this end that the verbatim or sections of tape-recordings, or transcripts of tapes, can be very helpful. In the answer to Question 1.6 we have described the verbatim, which is probably the fullest way apart from taping of presenting the detailed interaction of a counselling session. We address the use of tapes in the answer to Question 1.11, although we recognize in our answer that it is not possible to play back the whole session.

Generalized discussion of clients can yield only so much, and too often supervisees who do not prepare a verbatim or a tape only present rather sketchy information about the content of sessions. It is in the detail of what the client expressed, and what the therapist said and felt, that supervision gets closest to the therapeutic relationship. Such detail enables alternative responses to be framed, insightful interpretations to be recognized and subtle messages about the client's issues to be considered. It may not always be possible to write a full verbatim, or to use the facility of tape-recording, but recording as much as possible (including noting where one's memory has gone blank) is to be recommended. As we have noted already, these fuller notes do not have to be completed after every counselling session, only when it is envisaged that a session will be presented in supervision.

CHAPTER 2

The supervisee: further issues

2.1 I have just started to work in primary care, and I wonder whether I should change my supervisor, who has always been in independent practice and is, I think, not familiar with short-term contracts?

This question of matching supervisor to the type of supervision work is an important one, and it raises the question of whether supervisors need particular skills and a special knowledge base for specific settings and models or whether skills and knowledge are transferable across both theories and settings.

Certainly, short-term, brief or focused work (the terms are used interchangeably here) have a very different base and philosophy to long-term or open-ended contracts. Time is of the essence, so a focus is needed, goals are set, and the ending is not only in sight but also worked with from the very beginning (Molnos, 1995; Culley and Wright, 1997). In more exploratory approaches, care has to be taken to limit interventions to what can be managed safely worked with within the time, and always with an ultimate view of an agreed focus kept firmly and specifically in view. Working within a psychodynamic frame, great care has to be taken in managing the transference (Malan, 1963). Some approaches involve very specific interventions and techniques, for example cognitive–analytic therapy (Ryle, 1992) and dialectical behaviour therapy.

Because time is so central, whatever theoretical approach is used, thinking and intervention have to be relatively speedy. This has implications for supervisory style too, and for frequency of supervision. If supervision is monthly, much short-term work could be near its end before supervision begins, and particularly for a beginner in this type of work this could be very unsatisfactory. Supervision has to model the model: the work has to be actively tracked and thought about regularly so that strategies can be planned and monitored – whether these be psychodynamically or behaviourally based. Whatever the theoretical model, short-term work requires an intense input of work, thought and review from client, practitioner and supervisor alike. There is not the luxury of time to simply allow the process and relationship to develop at their own pace.

In this question, there is a suggestion that the current supervisor may not be familiar with short-term contracts. Pragmatically, the first move is to check this out. Independent practice does not necessarily preclude supervisors from having worked in this way. Many independent practitioners do a mixture of longer-term work and time-limited work, the latter for instance for EAPs (Employee Assistance Programmes). We might also expect supervisors themselves to be aware of their strengths and limitations. If they know a supervisee is changing her or his setting and style of work, we would hope they would review with her or him the appropriateness of continuing the supervision arrangements. What the counsellor needs in her or his new work, as well as what may be prescribed by the employer, should be carefully assessed and measured against the skills and knowledge base of the supervisor.

However, it may not be this simple. Some supervisees intentionally select a supervisor who is not specifically trained or experienced in their particular field or setting. This is especially likely if the supervisees are experienced and want the view of an outsider rather than that of someone on the inside of that setting. They like the challenge of a different slant to their work and are confident enough in their own skills to manage and utilize this (see Question 1.3 on models of supervision). But this is not the case with other supervisees who want to know that their supervisor has skills, knowledge and experience in the field they are working in (see, for example, Question 2.2 on working with abused clients). Another factor is that some supervisors are capable of using their skills transferably: they are open to other ways of working and thinking; they are interested in organizational dynamics and structures even if they do not work in them; they are committed to the public sector and understand its particular demands, stresses and strains even if their working experience has not been in that sector. Others are more tunnel-visioned, with a very definite sense of the superiority of their own model of therapy and supervision, and therefore (often on their own admission) are not sufficiently flexible to work across modalities.

If this is the first time the counsellor who asks this question has worked in primary care, he or she may well want a supervisor who is experienced in this or similar work, one who understands the rigour of short-term work, who can help them in assessing client suitability, who is familiar with identifying an appropriate and workable focus, and who can advise on the particular techniques of short-term work. Just as importantly, this supervisee needs a supervisor who does not see long-term or open-ended work as the gold standard, with short-term work as the poor relation; rather, the significance and value of short-term work need to be appreciated and validated, albeit recognizing that it is not a panacea and so is not applicable to every situation. Supervisors will assist the work greatly when they can help supervisees assess when it is appropriate and when it is not, can support them in this assessment and its implications, and can work alongside them to review and plan within the time limit. Similarly, a supervisor can be an enormous support when he or she appreciates the constraints and pressures of counselling in this context, understanding the workings of the structure of primary care as well as valuing the work.

Supervisors who are effective in supervising short-term work have parallels perhaps with those who are effective practitioners in short-term work. Not only do they need to understand the model, but they need to be able to relate well quickly and to have a therapeutic confidence, enthusiasm and belief in what they are doing – balanced by a realistic view of what the model cannot do. The supervisor, like the counsellor, needs to be able to tolerate limitations, accepting that it is necessary to leave some aspects of the person untouched; in other words, therapeutic perfectionism has no place in short-term work, although a little help can sometimes lead to a lot of change.

In summary, supervisors and counsellors in this field need to be resilient, to work relationally and cooperatively, to be capable of thinking and conceptualizing quickly, and of making interventions promptly without being invasive, destructive or inappropriate. They need to get people on side and focus on the task quickly without misusing their power or authority. Such is the type of supervisor this questioner might already have, or may need to seek.

* * *

2.2 My newest client has said that she was abused as a child. Should I, in this case, and in others where special knowledge is involved, seek additional supervision from someone with that type of experience and expertise?

As we have said in Question 2.1, it is a moot point whether supervision involves transferable skills or whether it requires a specialist knowledge base geared to the work being presented (Walker, 2003). While those who work in a specialist service (for example, for eating disorders or for survivors of abuse) may well select a supervisor with known expertise in that field, this is more complicated for those who work generically. Clients obviously present with a whole range of issues: finding different supervisors for different presentations would clearly be both unmanageable and undesirable.

What is crucial is that supervision is adequate and sufficient for the work being presented, and this is perhaps particularly important when working with survivors of abuse. The nature of the material can be emotionally extremely demanding and the dynamics of the work complex. A supervisor needs to understand and be able to work with these dynamics to help the supervisee work effectively and not be overwhelmed by the experiences being described by clients who have been abused. A supervisor also needs to be very aware of the potentially traumatizing nature of the work, recognizing when the supervisee is in danger of being adversely affected (Herman, 1992; Walker, 2004).

This question clearly arises from someone who is aware that working with this new client is already complex and who wonders whether the present supervisor has sufficient or appropriate experience to work with this situation. But it is also important to recognize that one powerful dynamic of working with survivors is a type of counter-transference where the counsellor does not feel good enough or adequate enough to respond sufficiently to the client's needs. This in turn can be projected onto the supervisor, who may be seen as not being good enough either. As the abused child can vainly hope that there is someone somewhere who understands, and for the rescue that does not come, so the survivor may consciously or unconsciously want this too from the counsellor, who in turn experiences a counter-transference reaction that can lead to the counsellor similarly wanting the supervisor to be a rescuer, although the supervisor, like the counsellor, cannot fulfil that precise role. So it is vital, when considering supervisory needs, that both these possibilities are explored, that is does the supervisor have sufficient skills and experience? And does the impact of the dynamics of the client–counsellor–supervisor relationship need to be examined (a possible example of parallel process; see Question 2.5). Supervisors need to be aware of the powerful dynamics that might be at play, while also realistically assessing their skills and knowledge, which include of course facilitating a discussion such as the one we raise here. As one of us has written elsewhere:

> Supervisors cannot be skilful in everything, and they need to acknowledge this honestly and explore the issue with supervisees in relation to their particular work. This is an obvious part of the initial contracting, but since needs and workloads change and develop, the supervisory match therefore needs to be an on-going consideration. (Walker, 2003: 129)

Supervisees also need to know that their supervisor can manage the material presented and will not be damaged by it. They need to feel sufficiently safe to unload and to share negative responses and feelings. One reason for seeking specialist or additional supervision in abuse work is where the counsellor does not feel sufficiently safe or where it is felt that the supervisor is not robust enough.

If counsellors come to the conclusion that they need additional supervision, this is obviously best done by mutual agreement between the supervisor and supervisee. If it is not possible to achieve such consensus, the supervisory relationship will inevitably become strained. There is, however, no reason why having different supervisors for different pieces of work cannot work well. Indeed, a supervisor may also suggest that it could be helpful to draw on another's expertise and knowledge, and to incorporate this in the ongoing supervision of that client.

Although some might feel that having two supervisors for the same client could be confusing and might encourage splitting (which is another possible dynamic in abuse work), this is not always the case. We know of instances where counsellors have found two views extremely helpful, accurately reflecting, in fact, different aspects of the work and of the client under discussion. This is more likely to be helpful with counsellors and therapists who have considerable experience, as they are more able to integrate different views, to manage uncertainty and to be more confident in sifting and sorting what is most relevant and helpful.

In that case, a crucial factor is ensuring clarity of boundaries: who is doing what and for whom and for how long? Seeking extra supervision needs to be set up as carefully as any regular supervisory contract. This is particularly so in abuse work, where the abuse of children involves an appalling invasion of all their boundaries and, potentially, ripples powerfully through all other relationships, including the therapeutic and the supervisory.

There are various models for seeking extra supervision. As noted above, the supervisor might suggest this, or the supervisor may seek extra help if supervising a complex case outside her or his normal expertise. It is important for supervisors to use others who have specialist knowledge to assist them in their work and role. The counsellor may choose to consult another supervisor on a single occasion over a specific issue or difficulty and then take this learning back into the usual supervision. Another alternative is when the regular supervisor continues to supervise but there is occasional, although regular, input from someone with particular expertise.

It may be that both supervisor and supervisee agree the case needs ongoing regular supervision elsewhere because of the specialized issues involved; we have known this to happen, particularly when the client is very dissociated or where there are aspects of satanic or ritual abuse, or abuse within a ring of abusers. Scott (1998: 83) describes how such supervision was a 'life saver' to her when she first worked with a ritual abuse survivor, reflecting the experience of many practitioners when they first encounter such horrors. It can be difficult for supervisors who do not have a degree of specialist knowledge to provide this level of support in such a difficult context. Perhaps the key is that the interest of the client must be paramount and that all parties involved hold this as their central tenet.

It can be difficult to locate specialist supervisors, particularly for those working in rural areas. It is, therefore, important to think creatively about how this might be obtained and managed. Telephone supervision is one possibility (see Question 4.5) or alternating the phone with face-to-face meetings. Another possibility, where there are colleagues who are working in the area of abuse, is peer-group supervision (see Question 2.7) or setting up a specialist supervision group, that is in addition to individual supervision. Both these options have the advantage of easing the isolation many feel when working with survivors of abuse (often a dynamic that reflects the isolation of the abused child). Such groups, even if they do not meet very frequently, can agree that colleagues are available for telephone support and discussion between sessions. Although we are not familiar with supervision via email, this may be another possibility for those living at a distance from a suitable specialist. Working with abuse, particularly if this is a large part of a practitioner's workload or if the case presents especially distressing or disturbing material, requires more support than supervision alone, and a wider support network is essential.

Taking on an abused client, even if this is for the first time, does not automatically mean that extra or specialist supervision is needed. Although working with survivors is often complex, the therapeutic needs of survivors vary, as does the complexity of what they need. However, supervisors and counsellors vary too, and finding a supervisory match that is sufficient for this work is not always straightforward: there are instances where perfectly good supervision simply cannot match a particular case. Recognizing that other expertise may be necessary in very complex work does not represent either failure or inadequacy; rather, it reflects maturity, common sense and professionalism.

Supervisors know that, however skilled they are, they cannot be everything to everybody – grandiosity is not in the best interests of either counsellors or clients. At the same time, supervisors, like counsellors, need to be aware that they can be caught up in the same dynamics of feeling helpless, useless and overwhelmed as their supervisees and abused clients. They too can feel overwhelmed, believing they have little help to offer. They have therefore to consider carefully whether they are caught up in this dynamic or they really do not have sufficient skill to manage it. If it is the former, the supervisory task is to contain and hold the frame and to work on identifying and understanding the powerful effects of the counter-transference. If the latter, other alternatives need to be considered. What is ultimately important is supervision that provides a safe and secure containment, which in turn enables counsellors to be effective in containing and working with their clients.

* * *

2.3   Is it wise to change supervisors every two years, in order to broaden experience?

It is often said that a change of supervisor every so often is important, and in many ways there is a good argument for doing so. However helpful a supervisor is (see Question 1.3), changing to another who is equally good usually provides a new perspective, partly because different interests will be brought into the discussion. Changing supervisors also provides the opportunity to work with therapists of each gender, with particular specialist experience (see Questions 2.1 and 2.2) and even of different orientations (see Question 1.3 and 4.4). Another possibility that needs to be considered is that changing supervisors can also mean changing to a different type of supervision, such as pairs' or group supervision (see Questions 4.6 and 4.7): this means not only a change of supervisor but also introducing the refreshment that comes from working with different colleagues.

However, there may be good reasons not to change, or not to change with such regularity. One is geographical location, which may mean that good supervisors are thin on the ground (although there is always the possibility of telephone supervision; see Question 4.5); a second is where the particular experience of the supervisor is necessary for the setting in which the supervisee works and where similar expertise is hard to locate within a reasonable distance (Questions 2.1. and 2.2); a third is where membership of a supervision group may require commitment to the group for a longer period for maximum effectiveness and where the inevitable changes in group membership mean that new elements are periodically introduced into the group, thereby refreshing its work; finally, experienced therapists or counsellors may get to the point where their supervisor is just right for them, where finding another supervisor with the same level of experience would be very difficult and change for the sake of change would be counter-productive. In any of these circumstances, and as long as the reason for staying with a supervisor is not an underlying collusiveness and cosiness, more of what is working appears to us to be a perfectly acceptable option.

* * *

2.4   I feel uncomfortable sometimes when my supervisor is critical of the client or tells me how I should tackle particular aspects of the work. Is this usual?

It is interesting how close this questioner's experience, which is not at all uncommon, is to a phrase in an article by Searles, where he describes the supervisee as 'feeling caught between the patient's intense criticism on the one hand, and the supervisor's disapproval on the other'(1962: 587). A 'patient's criticism' may not be obvious, but Searles implies that it is present as long as the therapist is not making her or him well. Yet there is also a conflation between client and counsellor here, because what we imagine this questioner feels is criticism both of self and of the client.

Supervision has a strange dynamic to it, in that probably the counsellor has developed not only empathy but also considerable sympathy for the client, while the supervisor, being at one remove, and not knowing the client personally, has a distance from the therapeutic situation. It is this that makes it possible for the supervisor to identify aspects of the client that the supervisee does not see; that is, after all, one of the purposes of supervision. But when a supervisor comments upon the client, especially about negative aspects that the supervisee may not have spotted, this can feel like an attack upon someone of whom the supervisee has grown somewhat fond (another word that Searles uses positively of the therapist–patient relationship).

So, while supervisors can be inappropriately critical or can appear so in the way in which they dissect the client's thoughts, feelings and actions, much of the difficulty is caused by the identification of supervisee and client: when a supervisor identifies an aspect of the client that the supervisee has not seen, the supervisor also implies some criticism of the counsellor.

Searles addresses this dynamic as one of the problems of supervision. He acknowledges that 'the fact that I perceive some aspect of the treatment situation which he has not seen does not mean that he [the supervisee] is stupid and I am intelligent' (1962: 588). He also observes that a very common experience in supervision is that 'when I point out to the student how he should have responded, without helping him to discover what factors in the patient's psychopathology made it difficult for him to respond, I do not actually help him; rather I only leave him feeling more wrong, stupid and inadequate than ever' (1962: 589). How reassuring this sentence is! Searles has identified an important factor in the therapeutic situation: that a therapist will often see one side of the picture, more commonly the side that the client wants the therapist to see, and, in spotting this, the therapist is less able to see another side: the therapist may, for example, pick up the sadness in the client, but fail to spot the anger, or identify what the client did wrong, without seeing that the client might have been trying to put something right, even if the attempt was doomed to fail. If the supervisor sees this other side, it is because the supervisor has the benefit of this more distant, but overall, perspective, just as both therapist and supervisor always have the benefit of hindsight.

Searles also draws attention to the competitiveness that is implicit in a supervisory relationship. As he puts it, 'supervision early involves an inarticulate kind of competition as to which of the two participants is to be the therapist to the other' (1962: 601), although this might be better understood by most supervisees and supervisors as which is to be the therapist to the client! Furthermore, Searles suggests that this competitiveness 'has at times appeared to me to be a defence against the student's and my being drawn together in compassion for the human being whose tragedies, so much of a piece with all human tragedy, we are trying to help him face and integrate' (1962: 601–602). He observes that much psychoanalytic training (his own orientation) is suspicious of compassion, seeing it as a reaction against 'a much more real and powerful underlying sadism' (1962: 602). To counter 'bonds of shared compassion' in supervision, which in the light of such teaching is felt to be bewildering, supervisor and supervisee 'resort to long familiar modes of reaction such as intellectual competitiveness in order to find relative comfort' (1962: 602).

There is then in the supervisory relationship one possible element, that of the competitiveness between supervisor and supervisee, as to which better understands and can help the client, a dynamic that the supervisor in particular always needs to be on guard against. As for the supervisee, there are always going to be times when self-criticism reinforces what a supervisor says, so that a failure to see an aspect of the client, or the correction of a weak response, is heard as more severe than it is meant. This is something that the supervisee always needs to be on guard against, an over-reaction against what the supervisor says, which can lead to unhelpful defensiveness of self or the client. See also the response to Question 3.9, where different dimensions of the anxiety that is inherent in the learning situation are described.

Searles (1962) paints a more positive picture of what supervision can become, setting out a goal to which both parties might aim:

> As the tensions in the relationship diminish and as the mutual and more explicit work concerning the patient proves increasingly successful, there develops an increasingly free give-and-take at this deeper level also. Not only does the student form constructive identifications with the supervisor, but the latter identifies with the former in those areas where the student manifests professional skills, and areas of emotional openness, beyond those

which the supervisor has previously achieved . . . . I strongly surmise that we are moving towards the day when there will be equally general agreement as to the essentially therapeutic significance, for both participants, of . . . supervision. (1962: 601–602)

* * *

2.5   My supervisor keeps mentioning 'parallel process'. What is that?

From time to time, a concept or a phrase catches on and proves to be a valuable idea, but such a concept can be overused, sometimes in the process drifting some way from its original meaning. An important concept may also extend its meaning over a period of time – counter-transference is an example, a term that relates to the concept of parallel process. At one time, counter-transference was used to describe the unhelpful reactions in the therapist to the client that might interfere with, or prevent, the understanding of the therapist. Later it was extended to include reactions in the therapist to the client that instead of being unhelpful prove to have potential value in understanding what the client is experiencing or how the client is trying to relate to the therapist. The danger, however, of this extension of meaning is that the earlier definition of counter-transference can get lost, so that therapists forget that their personal reactions may have two quite distinct causes: they may be occasioned by being with the client, and represent something that is relevant to the client, but they might still be intrusive reactions that simply belong to the therapist, and should not be attributed to the client.

The term 'parallel process' in summary means a possible parallel between what is experienced in supervision and what the supervisee experiences with the client. It was a highly informative idea when first mooted and one that increased the understanding of the relationship between the supervisory relationship and the therapeutic relationship with the client which the supervisee is describing. It remains as valuable an idea in supervision as when it was first identified, but there is a danger that some reactions in the supervisory process are attributed to parallel process and not to factors that are more related to the supervisor and/or the supervisee, rather than to the supervisee and the client. And although supervisors can use the term accurately, and helpfully, they can also apply it too often and indiscriminately.

To trace the development of the term, we need to go back over 50 years, to a breakthrough article by Searles, an American psychoanalyst, who worked much of the time with schizophrenic patients. His paper, 'The informational value of the supervisor's emotional experiences' (Searles, 1965:

157–76), introduced a number of novel ideas. Up to that time, there had been little concentration in psychoanalysis upon the emotional relationship between a supervisor and supervisee. The relationship was essentially seen as that of teacher and student, one that might engender certain feelings, but feelings that were likely to be of the type that would interfere with the supervisory process – fear of criticism, anxiety about presenting mistakes, rivalry with the teacher, etc. There might also be positive feelings such as one would expect in a relationship between colleagues. However, intense positive feelings were also seen as counter-productive, and likely to lessen the value of the supervision – undue admiration, for example, leading to compliance. Even around the time of Searles' article, another analyst (Keiser, 1956) had written of the emotional relationship in supervision in this rather straightforward way, indicating that the progress of the supervisee could by recognized by 'greater ease and facility in presenting to the supervisor, a diminution of blocks to his listening, his acceptance of supervision, a sharpened capacity to observe and awareness of his typical mistakes which he learns to avoid, and his application of well-timed interpretations'. Searles accepts this as a good description if we regard supervision simply as a learning situation, that is one where the student learns from the master, but he suggests, in a second paper on the same topic (1962), that he would want to add that supervision is about learning to depend less upon the supervisor and to assume more responsibility for the client. But for all this, Searles writes, this way of looking at supervision misses the 'subtle resonances to the progressing treatment situation' (1962: 596). There are additional ways of understanding what occurs in supervision, especially in the relationship between the supervisor and the supervisee.

We note that he does not suggest that these ways of understanding are the only feature of supervision, so it remains important for a supervisor to be alert for difficulties that can arise in the supervisory relationship, as it is also for a supervisee, who should try to discuss such difficulties if the supervisor fails to spot them (see Question 2.8). But there is, none the less, this other way of understanding difficulties and disturbances that arise – although we notice that what Searles stresses here are difficulties and disturbances, not anything and everything that occurs in supervision. His conception is an important one, that 'the supervisor experiences, over the course of a supervisory relationship, as broad a spectrum of emotional phenomena as does the therapist or even the patient himself – although to be sure, the supervisor's emotions are rarely as intense as those of the therapist, and usually much less intense than those of the patient' (Searles, 1955: 158). He is suggesting that the relationship between supervisor and supervisee may reflect the relationship between therapist and client, which in turn may reflect the internal world (and perhaps the external relationships) of the client.

Although Searles does not draw the parallel, this is a similar phenomenon in supervision to the concept of the 'living laboratory', first introduced by Freud as a way of describing how, through the transference in the therapeutic relationship, the therapist is able to catch glimpses of other relationships, often earlier ones, in the client's experience. Although transference is very similar, the more obvious parallel is counter-transference, since this helps us understand Searles' concept more clearly. The supervisor's emotional reaction or counter-transference to the supervisee, as it occurs from time to time, might provide clues to what is going on in the therapy. Just as Freud discovered that transference is not necessarily a hindrance to therapy, but provides a valuable resource, and just as Heimann (1950) and others said much the same about counter-transference, so Searles suggests that, if the relationship between the two or more people in supervision is disturbed by emotional reactions, this need not be felt to be anti-educational, interrupting the learning in supervision; it is both therapeutic and educational. We note too that, while Searles concentrates upon such disturbance of feelings on the part of the supervisor, he makes it clear that the disturbance can equally be in the supervisee as well.

Searles' 1955 paper describes this phenomenon as a 'reflection process' (1955: 159). This reflection process takes place partly because the supervisor is at a greater emotional distance from the patient than the therapist. In his 1962 paper, he writes:

> My potential usefulness springs in large part from the simple fact that I am at a greater psychological distance than is the student from the patient's psychopathology – specifically from the patient's anxiety and ambivalence. This greater distance leaves me relatively free from anxiety and able, therefore, to think relatively clearly and unconstrictedly. This position is mine, and this potential usefulness is mine, irrespective of whether, for example, in other situations the student may prove himself more intelligent than I, and a more effective practitioner than I. (Searles, 1962: 587)

This concept, as well as another important paper on a therapist's counter-transference feelings of love (Searles, 1959), influenced Janet Mattinson in Britain, although she refers to the process as 'mirroring' (1975). The term then seems to have spread through what was then called Marriage Guidance, which drew upon Mattinson's work. Quite where the term 'parallel process' arose, we find difficult to ascertain – the first references to it in relation to supervision seem to be in 1976 (Doehrman, 1976; Sachs and Shapiro, 1976). What is remarkable is that the term, which originates in psychoanalytic literature, has spread to many other orientations, some of which would not normally wish to be associated with psychoanalytic ideas.

Searles (1955) provides some helpful examples of what he means by the 'reflection process', both from individual and from group work:

1. He started to supervise a therapist whose work he respected, but he was surprised in the first session to hear the therapist describing his work with a client, because it was work which Searles felt, as indeed the therapist felt, was poor. While he described the incident, the therapist looked at Searles searchingly, as though expecting criticism, and indeed he got it, because Searles felt it and expressed it. Searles was especially troubled when the second session contained a detailed description of another situation with the same client, which was clearly anti-therapeutic. He again felt strong condemnation of the therapist and began to wonder whether he could go on with supervising him if he was going to have such strong feelings. He was just thinking this when the therapist told him that one of the things he noticed about his client was that he kept presenting material which might be called ugly – perverse sexual material, things about faeces, etc. – and how the client, in speaking about this, looked searchingly at the therapist. Searles was then able to point out the similarity between the therapist's reporting to him and the patient's reporting to the therapist, and drew the inference from his own feelings that the client was trying to maintain a distance between himself and the therapist. We note that, while Searles alludes to the similarity in the way both therapist and client looked, he appears not to have said that he felt like distancing himself from the therapist (1955: 160–161).

2. After several months of supervision, a therapist was quoting the client, and the material was, as usual, quite confusing. As the therapist spoke, Searles fantasized that the therapist was asking for a declaration of love by Searles towards him. He dismissed this as irrelevant, only a few minutes later to hear him quote the client as saying something that sounded like the disguised expression of romantic love for her therapist. Searles' own reaction a minute before enabled him to spot this, under the disguised expression, and suggest an interpretation, which in turn enabled the sexual nature of the transference and counter-transference to become clearer. Again, we note he does not appear to have shared his own fantasy with the therapist, but if he had not experienced that fantasy he, like the therapist, might have missed the allusion (1955: 164–165). He notes that negative feelings, as in the first example, and positive feelings as in the second, are both sometimes carried over into the supervisory process.

3. He gives another example of being in supervision himself and feeling uncomfortable with what his supervisor was suggesting, even though intellectually he could see the sense of it. He then realized that this was also the way his patient reacted to him: being intolerant of his saying anything to her (1955: 167).

4. He also gives examples from group supervision, such as the members of the group reflecting the relationship between therapist and patient in

feeling very sleepy just as the therapist felt sleepy (1955: 169), and the members failing to understand one another, reflecting the sense of disintegration in the client being presented (1955: 170–171).

Searles cannot explain this phenomenon, although he thinks it is triggered by unconscious identification. He observes that the emotion and depth of emotional involvement is most intense in the client and only slightly less intense in the therapist-client relationship, but it is more diluted in the relationship between therapist and supervisor; it is perhaps less threatening and, therefore, a little more easily spotted, even if the client or the supervisee is unaware of it. We wonder ourselves whether, because supervision is usually less intense than therapy, a supervisor is someone who can be more in touch with her or his own unconscious, and with her or his emotional reactions, however bizarre. This is even more than the therapist is capable of being, partly because it is much safer to be in touch with the unacceptable when the client is at one remove. The emotional reactions of the supervisor, therefore, may be more readily monitored, to see if they are saying something about the client or the relationship between the supervisee and the client.

It is in this sense that supervisors use the phrase, although they too often observe, in a way that we are fairly sure the pioneers of the concept did not: 'Ah, look at the parallel process here.' Sometimes they are right, that it is possible to extrapolate from what is being experienced in the supervision to what might be part of the therapeutic relationship or of the inner world of the client. What concerns us, however, is the way in which parallel process has almost in some circles become a mantra, cited in virtually every supervision session, especially by psychodynamic practitioners. There is that other explanation for emotional disturbances in the supervisory relationship, which needs equal attention: just as with the concept of counter-transference we always have to remember that a therapist's feelings with a client may be the therapist's issue, not the client's, so what is experienced within supervision may belong only to supervision!

Searles is also cautious about the reflection process, writing that what the therapist reports by way of interactions with the client may, in fact, be a reflection of the supervisory relationship. He observes the two-way process involved in supervision: that just as what is happening in the therapy can be imported into the supervision so what is happening in the supervision can be exported to the therapy. In his 1962 paper, 'Problems of psycho-analytic supervision', he writes that as the therapist–supervisor relationship changes for the better so too does the therapeutic relationship:

Supervision early involves an inarticulate kind of competition as to which of the two participants is to be the therapist for the other; subsequently, as the tensions in the relationship diminish and as the mutual and more explicit work concerning the patient proves increasingly successful, there develops an increasingly free give-and-take at this deeper level also. (Searles, 1962: 601)

But he also says in his 1955 paper that, if there is more anxiety in the therapist–supervisor relationship than in the therapist–client relationship, this can get transferred into the therapist–patient relationship, and so give rise to disturbing processes. This inevitably leads to a complex process: at times a supervisee may report interactions with the client that are, in fact, a reflection of the supervisory relationship. This possibility is echoed by Langs (1979), who suggests that the supervisor should hear the comments made by the client, and reported by the supervisee, as first potentially referring to herself or himself (that is, the supervisor), next to the supervisee and only then as the client talking about self or others. Jones (1989) provides an interesting example of a client reported as saying she felt bruised, and that this might have been a reference to the way that Jones, as a supervisor, had tried to pressure his supervisee over her handling of this client's lateness, himself thus bruising the supervisee (1989: 509).

This is an important qualification, because some supervisors, in Jones' position, would have said: 'The way I bruised you must have come unconsciously from this client's wish to bruise you by being late – that's parallel process.' But it is not. It is a parallel situation, surely, but not parallel process in the sense that Searles and others mean it.

We would wish to extend Langs' advice on how to hear the client's comments, so that a supervisor should also listen to a supervisee's comments as first potentially referring to herself (or himself), next to the therapist–client interaction, and only then to the client talking about self and others. One of us was once supervising an experienced therapist, who was talking about a client who was persistently late. She had been so ever since a recent session in which the therapist felt the client had expressed deep feelings about her dying partner. The therapist found herself very angry with the client for her lateness, fuming during the minutes she was kept waiting, and thinking she could be doing something better with her time: indeed, she could have been visiting another of her clients, who was in hospital. For a while the supervision concentrated upon a reported session where things had, through the therapist's careful interpretation, suddenly gone very deep for her client. The supervisor suggested the therapist might refer to the relationship with her client rather than concentrate, as she was, on interpreting the client's material as purely referring to her dying partner. The client's references to poison in the atmosphere could, of course, be interpreted as the poison in her partner's body, but might they not also be about the poisonous feeling the client felt for the therapist, for taking her so deep into her most painful feelings?

The supervisor suggested to the therapist that it was important to work with these disguised references to their therapeutic relationship: only when the client's relationship with the therapist had been rendered less dangerous could the therapist again try to help the client reach into those painful feelings about her partner's inevitable death. But the supervisor remembered, while saying this, that there was this other layer, which Langs had referred to, and suddenly saw how the therapist's anger with the lateness of her client was possibly related to the fact that the supervisor had also turned up late for – in fact, nearly forgot about – the previous supervision session. Instead of pursuing the therapist–client reference, the supervisor therefore wondered how much the therapist's anger with her client, which she admitted was over the top, was also anger with the supervisor for being late. The therapist responded that she recognized that anyone can make a mistake and that she forgot about sessions from time to time and therefore understood why the supervisor had been late (which, indeed, she had said at the time). But she admitted that she would have been very angry indeed if the supervisor had not turned up at all, because she was desperate to talk about the client she had mentioned being in hospital, since she was desperately worried about how to handle that situation, and there was indeed still a residue of anger for being kept waiting and in suspense. This then made sense of her opening remark in the current session, an apparently casual aside, that she had set her alarm clock wrong and had arrived at her therapist's (whom she saw the hour before supervision) 75 minutes early!

Langs' idea strengthens the counter-balance that we already detect in Searles. How the supervisor and supervisee feel, relate and behave in the supervision may reflect the client. But equally so what the supervisee says about the client may reflect how the supervisee experiences the supervisor. The following is a disguised example from a practice session on a supervision training course:

> Jill is supervising Jack. Jack starts by saying that he is getting nowhere with a bulimic client, and he is puzzled. Jill interrupts in the first minute and asks how Jack relates to the client, but Jack interrupts her by saying that the client had seen a counsellor before and stopped after two sessions. He goes on to say how outwardly well adjusted the client appears and how difficult it is to get beneath that. Jill keeps quiet for a while but interrupts again three minutes later when Jack talks about the client not coming to see him for a while, and Jack quickly in turn interrupts her and talks about other breaks in the therapy. He says that part of him feels very irritated by the client. She talks and talks and he can't say anything. (Might he be referring to Jill here?) About 10 minutes later, during which time Jill has spoken briefly every minute or so, Jack says how every session with this client he attempts to stop her talking so much. She fills the session and keeps him at a distance. 'I let her control me by her incessant talking,' he says. (Again, is he talking about

Jill?) Jill wonders whether he could stop the client and focus on something. The supervision session goes on. Jill intervenes every minute or two, looking at the way the client keeps missing sessions and how the client is avoiding looking at herself. After about twenty minutes, she says to Jack, 'There's so much there – such a huge amount – and yet you're not given an opportunity. It must be frustrating'. Jack says, 'Well, in her sweet way she puts me under tremendous pressure.'

What is happening in this practice supervision session? Those who favour an interpretation of parallel process may want to say that supervision is paralleling therapy, with the supervisor and the therapist interrupting each other, and perhaps the supervisor particularly identifying unconsciously with the client, so that it is actually difficult for Jack to get a word in edgeways. The supervisor fills the session, perhaps like the client also fills herself with food, and keeps Jack's case at a distance. This was indeed what Jill said when the practice session was reviewed. Alternatively, it could be said, as Langs might, that the supervisor, hardly before the session has got going, interrupts Jack, and that thereafter Jack talks about the client as breaking up the therapy and not giving it a chance to work, because that is what the supervisor is doing to him. Much of what Jack says could refer as well to the supervisor as to the client. In this particular session, our preference is to accept the 'Langsian' interpretation of what might be going on, rather than a potentially reflective or parallel process.

This is only one of several cautionary notes about an extremely popular concept. Searles, like Mattinson, does not concentrate upon overt feelings but on picking up clues as to unconscious material, as yet not seen by client or therapist and only dimly or quickly glimpsed by the supervisor. Too often, parallel process is used to describe things that are staring the supervisory pair in the face. There is little subtlety about it, as there is in Searles. In practice, too, we also note that such perceptions occupy only a small part of supervisory hours, although when they occur they offer clues to obscure yet highly relevant areas that trouble the therapeutic relationship. Parallel process does not happen all the time. Another caution should be noted in how Searles uses his emotional reactions: 'Incidentally, I am not advocating the supervisor's emoting, in an overt fashion, to the supervisee. I am focusing upon the supervisor's "subjective" emotional experience in the supervisory situation' (1955: 158n). We see him storing away his observation until, as in therapy itself, there is another communication that provides some confirmation.

Finally, Searles makes it quite clear towards the end of his 1955 paper that supervisors still have to consider whether there may be some other explanation for their emotional reactions; for example, a supervisor may be projecting an important part of her or his own personality onto the therapist *and* the patient, and not unnaturally seeing a parallel, whereas in each case what is seen belongs to the supervisor rather than to each of them. Bearing in mind the closeness between disturbances in the supervisor and counter-transference, Searles also points to the possibility that the phenomenon he describes, of supervision apparently mirroring therapy, may sometimes be a form of classic counter-transference, in which the therapist responds to the client and supervisor in the same way: not surprisingly, there is a parallel process, but it is nothing to do with the client.

We have examined this concept at length because in our opinion it is one that is overused in supervision and, as a result, becomes less valuable for being watered down. If it is seen everywhere, it teaches us little. We also want to identify the number of different explanations there may be for what is experienced in the supervision session. Indeed, if we have the following permutations right, it may be necessary to consider that, as the supervisor listens to the therapist describing the session with the client, what the supervisor (and perhaps the supervisee) experiences may be:

(a) what the therapist feels with the client
(b) what the client feels with the therapist
(c) what the therapist feels with significant others
(d) what the client feels with significant others
(e) what the therapist feels with the supervisor
(f) what the supervisor feels with the therapist
(g) what the supervisor feels with significant others
(h) what the supervisor feels about the client.

No wonder Zinkin (1988: 19), after Freud, calls supervision 'the impossible profession'!

* * *

2.6   I have worked for many years as a counsellor and am currently cutting down on the number of people I see – is it therefore all right for me to cut down on the amount of supervision I am used to receiving?

We address a similar question to this in Question 1.4, where we suggest that the amount of supervision a practitioner receives depends to some extent upon their own needs – such as the amount of experience they have, the setting in which they are working and the number of clients they are seeing.

The short answer to this question is, therefore, that it appears the right step to take to cut down on supervision proportionate to the client load. Nevertheless, we are aware that the practitioner's professional association may have clear rules – such as that which is in place (as we write) for BACP-accredited counsellors and therapists, where an hour-and-a-half of individual supervision is required (or equivalent times in group supervision, see Question 2.8). Several writers on supervision have questioned the need for such strict regulations in the case of experienced therapists and counsellors, and particularly when experienced therapists cut down their practice (Jacobs, 2000; Shipton, 2000; Wheeler, 2000). We are not aware whether other associations are less stringent to qualified members who are reducing the number of hours of client contact. The only alternative in these circumstances for BACP-accredited members is to let accredited status drop, while remaining a member of BACP, and still adhering to the less precise definition in the 'Ethical Framework' (2002) of 'regular and ongoing supervision'. A BACP information sheet on supervision suggests that 'in the exceptional case of a well-trained, highly experienced but unaccredited counsellor undertaking a light caseload . . . the assessment of sufficient supervision [might] dip below the baseline' (BACP, 1998: 3).

This is also a matter that could be discussed with the present supervisor, whose knowledge of the therapist's practice and level of experience will assist a more objective assessment to be made.

* * *

2.7   A colleague and I think we might form a group for peer supervision. Is peer supervision adequate? What helps it to be effective?

Is it adequate?

Here we need to take into account the level of experience of the questioner. It is also not clear if these counsellors intend having other forms of supervision or whether peer supervision is the only method available to them.

For new practitioners, and when undergoing training, peer supervision would not be adequate, and reputable training courses would certainly demand supervision individually, in pairs or in a small group with an experienced practitioner and supervisor facilitating the process (or sometimes a combination of these). Similarly, many agencies require this level of supervision.

So there is a question of when peer supervision might be appropriate and helpful and for whom. Peer supervision works best for practitioners who are experienced, both in their own practice and in the receiving and possibly the provision of supervision. This is certainly the case when it is the only supervision being considered. For it to work best, all those involved need to be used to supervision as a process and preferably used to taking part in groups.

Peer supervision for those who are not very experienced can be a very helpful adjunct to other forms of supervision, although there needs to be clarity in terms of its purpose and boundaries (for example, which cases are taken to which supervision?).

In order for peer supervision to work, it is crucial to have certain basics in place. Establishing the time and timing is essential: how long the group will meet at each session, how often will it meet, as well as agreement on starting and ending promptly. Having an appropriate room that is always available, confidential and of a sufficient size is important. If the room is in an agency and has to be booked and paid for, there needs to be clarity regarding who is responsible for making the arrangements and how the room is to be funded.

The group members must be committed to this type of supervision and prepared to put this commitment into practice by prioritizing the time and ensuring regular attendance. If the group is taking place in an organizational context, it is crucial to ensure that the organization has agreed and understood any implications in terms of organizational issues, particularly those of resources it may need to supply, and ensuring that staff will be free to attend. The organization needs to provide real support rather than tokenistic agreement. It is worth taking time in the early stages of forming the group to encourage potential members to seriously consider if they really want to give time and energy to the group and to encourage everyone to note and explore any ambivalence they may have.

Similarly, it is worth exploring what everyone wants and expects from the group, examining whether their goals and needs are realistic and compatible. For instance, if someone wants to join a peer group because they are unhappy with their existing supervision arrangements, they may need to resolve that first. Clarity of purpose and commonality of need and aims give a good chance of success. The group may decide its purpose is occasional reflection, or as an ongoing process of growth and development or as a meeting place for practitioners who already have a common core to their work and want to focus on this, such as those working in a particular modality (for example, focused or time-limited counselling), or working with a particular client group or presenting problem (for example, eating disorders or bereavement).

Other issues need to be decided at the formative stage. The size of the group needs to be large enough to allow for creative and effective use of group (see Question 4.7 on methods of working in a group). If the group adopts the model discussed below of the members taking it in turn to facilitate the group, it needs to have sufficient members to allow it to operate as a group when one of them is 'outside' the group as the facilitator. However, it also needs to be of a size that gives members sufficient time to present their work, especially if it is their only source of supervision.

The size of the group is significant in deciding how often it meets and for how long, for example if it meets weekly for an hour and a half to two hours, and members of the group are at a similar level of experience, eight is a manageable number (two can present each week and everyone thereby presents once a month – although bear in mind the BACP guidelines for the necessary amount of supervision for accredited counsellors; see Question 2.8). This number allows plenty of potential for using role-play and other experiential methods, and for using group members as observers of such exercises. However, if the group meets only monthly, a smaller number is likely to work better, although it has to be recognized that this relates to the agreed and negotiated purpose of the group.

Eight people meeting monthly may be sufficient if the group has a very tightly defined and specific purpose, for example to consider issues arising from supervising on a training course. In that context, the main aim is principally to ensure that supervisors meet with one another and have a forum to which any questions or difficulties can be brought. However, if there is no such specific task, and the group's purpose is to explore cases, infrequent meetings inevitably mean less depth in the discussion, less continuity, more difficulty in creating group cohesiveness, greater likelihood of content and detail being forgotten, and the process being harder to monitor and reflect upon.

As with any other group, a peer-supervision group needs time to establish and settle – what is sometimes known as 'forming' and 'norming' (which may even include some 'storming'). Clarity and agreement as to how the time will be used gives a greater possibility of success. One model is to set aside unallocated time at each meeting, perhaps 15 minutes, for any concerns or urgent issues members who are not formally presenting may have. It is always surprising how much helpful work the group can do in a short space of time, and such a space lessens the anxiety that might otherwise interfere in the group process if anyone has a pressing difficulty. If there are no issues, this time can either be used by the agreed presenters or be used at the end to reflect on how the group has worked. If a group runs for an hour and a half, two people can present, with 15 minutes for the open agenda. A two-hour session gives even greater flexibility, but whatever time is chosen it is important to think carefully how best it can be used.

Deciding beforehand on who presents on each occasion provides a structure that is containing for the group. Rather than deciding this on a session-by-session basis, it is better if a rota of presenters is negotiated and agreed upon well in advance; it saves time and ensures that all involved know they have their fair share of time. If an individual presenter is unable to present on the designated day, it must be her or his responsibility to arrange to exchange sessions with another presenter. Having a unstructured group where everyone just brings something along when they feel like it may not work well. It appears democratic and collegial, but it easily dissolves into an unsatisfying, unsatisfactory experience and a wasteful use of time.

What helps a peer group to be effective?

Before setting up a peer group, it is worth giving time to consider the factors that might provide the peer group with the best chance of working effectively and check whether these are in place. Clear ground rules, a real commitment and enthusiasm are crucial. A peer group that is seen as second or third best, or as a cheap option, is not sufficient reason for joining one or starting one. As stated above, starting and ending on time and ensuring there are no interruptions are basic requirements, for example mobile phones must be turned off. The room must be booked so that there is no possibility of interruption. It is very disconcerting in the midst of discussion if someone comes in expecting the room to be free. Confidentiality and responsibility, as in all forms of supervision, need to be agreed, as does a policy on contacting other members for advice between sessions if it should be necessary. Since the peer group is unlikely to have an external facilitator, it is useful to agree on one member acting in this role each time. This person can act as timekeeper but can also help the group itself in its work, observing more objectively and recognizing process issues and themes. In rotating this role, no one member is either overburdened or labelled in that role; acting in this way also provides an opportunity for group members to develop their group-facilitation skills.

Each member needs to take responsibility for participating but not dominating, by giving feedback in a clear, constructive way and by being respectful to others, especially where opinions differ. Peer groups work best where members have some insight into their own part in the group, although the facilitator might be able to provide some feedback in this respect.

Those whose turn it is to present need to give some thought to what they want from the supervision, to come prepared and to take the task seriously. Maintaining a high level of interest in the group is another factor, for example presenters can choose the method by which they would like to be supervised (see Question 4.7). It can be helpful to have agreement on the option of occasional consultation with a trusted external facilitator, to help the group reflect on its work. Recording the sessions through a method that allows the group to quickly remember a case that has been discussed before prevents time being wasted in repeating old information (see Questions 1.11, 1.12 and 3.4 on recording supervision sessions).

What factors hinder a peer group working effectively?

The lack of clear purpose and commitment and meeting infrequently prevent a group from taking off in the first instance: it cannot form its own culture. Not having a designated facilitator makes it very difficult for some groups to maintain the task. If problems arise and there is no facilitator to take responsibility for exploring them, the group can flounder – this type of supervision is very demanding of the group, and it may encounter difficulties that are too problematic. Where peer groups do not deal with conflict, difference and disagreement constructively, or become collusive and deny difficulties, this prevents effective working. So do boundaries and ground rules that are either insufficiently clarified at the beginning or are broken without this being acknowledged, discussed and dealt with, for example people arriving late or not being properly prepared when presenting. Poor and unsuitable accommodation is another common hindering factor, as is a lack of clarity about whose responsibility it is to ensure this is in place. An organization that purports to be supportive but in reality is not (or even worse is sabotaging), and thereby fails to give real or adequate support, can also prevent the group effectively forming in the first place, or lead to its falling at the first hurdle. Some organizations may pressure staff into peer-group supervision without ensuring this is either what they want or what they need, just because it seems like a cheap option.

Peer supervision provides an excellent means for the sharing of ideas and experience, and for gaining a range of emotional, theoretical and clinical responses to work with clients. Many practitioners work in isolation, so that it can be a real privilege to be allowed to share in the work of others and to integrate a wider range of experience and perspectives. In terms of its sufficiency, this depends on the level of experience of the practitioner, the needs and demands of any employing agency, and the requirements of the professional association to which the counsellor or therapist belongs. There is, therefore, no clear answer to whether peer supervision provides enough supervision: it is for some and not for others, depending on the different factors discussed above and, of course, on the size and complexity of individual counsellors' workloads. Heron notes that peer supervision is 'invariably committed to transformation, either in the sense of enhancing the value that is present, or manifesting the value that is absent' (1993: 159). This enhancement is certainly the experience of many who participate in peer groups where they are carefully thought through, where ground rules are clearly established and agreed in the initial stages, and where they are carried through thereafter.

* * *

2.8   I have been offered the alternative of group supervision, having been used to seeing my supervisor one to one. What are the advantages and disadvantages of that, and how does it affect the number of hours I need to be supervised each month?

Sometimes group supervision is necessary because of the shortage of supervision in an agency – and this solution to the problem can therefore easily imply that group supervision is second best to individual or pairs' supervision. We are firmly convinced that group supervision is a different experience – and therefore no better and no worse than individual supervision. We set out in the answer to Question 4.7 just how rich an experience a supervision group can provide, enabling ways of using the material presented that is just not possible in individual work.

To some extent the advantages and disadvantages depend upon the size of the group that this therapist is being offered. If it is a group of three (which is what is sometimes defined as a group, since the supervisor obviously makes a fourth), the question of presentation time is not as important as it is in a larger group. Therefore, if the counsellor wants, or needs, the amount of time that he or she has been used to in one-to-one supervision, a smaller group is clearly a disadvantage, and a larger group a non-starter. Weighed against having less time to present, however, is the advantage of being able to listen to accounts of the work of other counsellors, and being able to make a contribution to their work. Not only does this then foster supervision skills, but, through working with others, different situations are reviewed that have or may have bearing on the counsellor's own practice. There is also the value that comes from a larger support group. When presenting, there are more than just the facilitating supervisor's views to play with, as well as more opportunity of learning from others who can share similar experiences from their work.

Also to be considered is that group or individual supervision do not have to be alternatives. It may be possible to use both, and, indeed, if the counsellor or therapist is accredited by BACP, it may be necessary to have both as is shown by the formula below for calculating the amount of supervision time a group provides towards fulfilling requirements.

The guidelines provided by BACP at the time of writing may be helpful if it comes to calculating whether or not practitioners moving into group supervision meet their profession's or organization's requirements. Where counsellors and therapists are in group supervision, their individual/equivalent time is calculated as follows.

Supervision groups of four members or fewer

Those in a supervision group of four members or fewer may claim half the time spent in the group per month as individual/equivalent time (e.g. if the group meets for three hours per month, half of this time (i.e. 1.5 hours) may be claimed as individual/equivalent supervision time).

Supervision groups of five members or more

Those in a supervision group of five members or more should divide the time spent in the group per month by the number of members in the group, excluding the facilitator or supervisor (e.g. if a group of six members meets for three hours per month, 30 minutes (three hours divided by six members) may be claimed as individual/equivalent supervision time).

Therefore, if the questioner is a BACP-accredited counsellor and joins a group of six members that meets twice a month for 90 minutes, a further hour's individual supervision each month will be necessary. Only if a larger group met weekly would it be sufficient on its own.

* * *

2.9 I am not very happy with the supervision I am receiving, but when I try to raise this with my supervisor she tells me it is because I have issues with her as an authority figure and I should take it to my own therapy. I think it's because I don't find her very effective. How can I resolve this?

Inevitably, there will be aspects of the supervisory relationship that relate to issues of authority (see also Question 3.9). Indeed, to be effective as a supervisor it is a necessary asset to be able to hold authority by having professional confidence, by being able to manage and contain difficult material and feelings, by being able to challenge constructively and by having sufficient self belief. There is, of course, a huge difference between holding authority in this positive sense and being authoritarian. Therefore, there is a considerable responsibility on supervisors not to misuse the explicit and necessary authority that is inherent in their role.

Yet supervisors need to acknowledge that related to authority they also have power. This can be in a very obvious sense, through being required to comment on their supervisees' work for purposes of their training or for accreditation by professional organizations. In addition, supervisees – especially those new to the process – can feel very vulnerable in exposing their work to someone identified as more skilled and experienced than they are; this inevitably creates a power imbalance. Supervisors do not put their own work on the line for the supervisee to scrutinize.

However, power exists on another level too when the supervisor can be experienced parentally and is thereby invested by the supervisee with considerable power and authority, with supervisees then potentially experiencing themselves as childlike and dependent. The extent to which this latter dynamic is seen as inherent, intrinsic and unavoidable depends largely on the theoretical perspective of the supervisor. The power and presence of the supervisor as a parental figure are far more likely to be seen as at the core of the process by psychoanalytically trained supervisors. But even within that tradition there will be more or less emphasis placed on this aspect, with some supervisory styles actively promoting such a dynamic while others are more collegial and open, thereby serving to minimize it. Similarly, some supervisees, because of their own histories, can more easily fall into experiencing supervisors as parental. Experience can also play a part, since new practitioners perhaps have a greater need for someone to fulfil this parental role. As Stoltenberg and Delworth (1987) discuss, the power and authority of supervisors can create feelings of inferiority in supervisees, and this power can be misused. They note that 'the supervisory relationship is one of inherently unequal status, power and expertise' (1987: 168).

These points provide a backdrop to this question. In this situation we appear to have a counsellor or therapist attempting to explore with the supervisor her or his unease with the supervision. This step is both mature and professional and one we would advise as a first step. But the response of the supervisor here has been to label this query as an authority issue. This may have its origins outside the sessions, presumably in the history of the supervisee; perhaps in the supervisor's view the authority issue is being transferentially experienced and expressed, therefore belonging in the therapy room and not in the supervisory relationship. Of course, the supervisee needs to consider and reflect on the accuracy of this supposition, but if he or she has reflected in this way and is sufficiently sure that it is not the case, or at least not the complete story, the supervisee is quite correct in wishing to question and challenge what the supervisor is saying.

This situation may suggest the flavour of a supervisor hiding behind theoretical rhetoric, rather than using theory to the advantage and benefit of supervisee and client. It is potentially a terrible trap for the supervisee: if there were not authority issues with the supervisor in the first instance, it is highly likely they will have now developed. In the same way, psychoanalytic interpretations about denial that are not accepted by the client can similarly contain an element of self-fulfilling prophecy. A client who rejects an interpretation of angry feelings towards their therapist is quite reasonably likely to become angry if the therapist is overpersistent in interpreting the anger. This dynamic is infantilizing in the extreme, and potentially abusive, whether it is a therapist or a supervisor who refuses to take on board the client's or the supervisee's concern about the process and discuss it fully and openly.

It appears that the supervisee in this case is in therapy, although clearly not all supervisees are. Supervisors cannot assume that any difficulties in a supervisory relationship can simply be sidelined in this way. If there are authority issues, the supervisor may be the direct cause of them rather than their being transferential in nature. Supervisors demonstrate unconscious patterns of relating, too, which can be unhelpful or destructive. At times (and we obviously hope for most of the time), their style will be helpful, but at other times (again we hope only occasionally, but they are human!), their style will be unhelpful; sometimes their knowledge and experience base will be sufficient, sometimes not. If the problem lies more with the supervisor than the supervisee, we would want to stress that it is not acceptable for supervisors to duck difficulties, or deny their own part in them, by playing games around power and theory (see Hawthorne, 1975).

This supervisee should obviously first raise this concern one more time with the supervisor, but, if there is no way of looking at the issue constructively, a change of supervisor should be considered, if this is possible. As long as the supervisee has carefully reflected on her or his own dynamic, and has made every attempt to resolve the issue with the supervisor, staying in that particular dyad risks being invalidated, demoralized and deskilled. Because counsellors and therapists are so used to struggling with difficult dynamics and issues with their clients, and work so hard on these, it is easy to fall into the same pattern with a supervisor. However, difficult clients may have to be struggled with, but unsatisfactory supervision in the final analysis does not. The relationship in supervision is very important, but, if it becomes the main concern, the supervision will fail to meet its main purpose.

But change may not be possible. If this supervisor has been selected by an agency or by a training course, the counsellor's autonomy may be more limited. In that instance, the only step left after raising it with the supervisor seems to be discussing the dilemma with a course tutor or line manager.

CHAPTER 3

The supervisor: initial questions

3.1 Is it useful to seek training to be a supervisor? Is there really that much that I need to learn?

Training for the role of supervisor is relatively new. Before the advent of training courses, the accepted progress of a therapist was that at a certain point of experience and seniority that person would become a supervisor. The supervisor's role was seen as a straightforward one, which more than anything else needed sufficient experience to have built up knowledge of practice as well as of the issues that clients by and large present. Indeed, when we once invited a very experienced supervisor to work on one of our courses, that person expressed the view that training was unnecessary, since everything that can be learned about supervision will have been learned through being in supervision.

We might agree to some extent with this, although we are aware that some supervisors, unlike the person we approached, do not present a good model of supervision, and so it is possible that the mistakes and shortcomings then go on to be reproduced in the supervisee who in turn takes on the supervisory role. But we also cannot agree, because, like the whole discipline of therapy and counselling, there is so much to be learned from someone else observing and commenting on our thoughts and behaviours, as supervisors as much as when therapists in supervision. And, if therapists are useful because they provide that other perspective for clients, trainers are useful in helping supervisors, and those wishing to become supervisors, to put their practice under the microscope. That is why in our own training of supervisors we have always placed most emphasis on the learning that comes from practice sessions, as well as from tapes of actual supervision sessions.

As a result, we have been able, with the cooperation of trainee supervisors, to draw up a profile of the competencies and other qualities that are probably important to develop. In reproducing that profile, we do not suggest that all these qualities are necessary before a supervisor can be seen as competent but that the different items identified represent the goal towards which supervisors should be working in honing their skills. Some aspects are perhaps more relevant to psychodynamic practice, since that is the orientation most of our work is concerned with. But equivalent areas of specific knowledge might be identifiable in other orientations.

We suggest there are four areas of competence that need to be addressed: knowledge, skills, qualities and requirements. It is, of course, debatable whether qualities can be learned through training if they are not in evidence in the first place, but they are qualities that can be developed.

As regards the *knowledge* base that a supervisor needs to have and be working to extend, we would want to stress that a thorough understanding of at least one theoretical model is vital, and some knowledge of a range of others (or at least of their most important features) is desirable, particularly if a supervisor is working with supervisees who come from a number of different trainings, or when working with integrative therapists. This wider knowledge encourages different formulations and conceptualizations of the material presented to be considered. An understanding of a relevant model of psychopathology is also important, especially when assisting in the assessment of potential clients for supervisees. In most supervision, knowledge of brief therapy, and when it is and is not appropriate to use it, is now essential. It is also important to have a working knowledge of professional ethics, with detailed knowledge of at least one code of ethics and practice – something that would be expected in any case of every practitioner for application in their own work. We also think it desirable that there is awareness of legal issues and of the literature that might be consulted when legal issues arise, for example the companion volume in this series by Jenkins et al. (2004). Similarly, a supervisor needs to be aware of the sociopolitical context of the supervisees, including equal-opportunities' issues, which means a working knowledge of issues around gender, race, disability, etc. (see Question 4.8).

Since a supervision contract is desirable, identification of what might need to be included in such a contract is important (see Question 3.2). Particular knowledge is necessary of the agency or the course that the supervisee comes from, including the policies of the agency with respect to child protection and mental-health legislation, and in relation to courses such knowledge should include the procedures for assessment (see Question 3.3). The other area of knowledge that may be necessary (although it is obviously a skill too) is of group dynamics, which applies, of course, to group supervision and to ways of using such a group effectively (see Questions 3.11 and 4.7).

Many of the *skills* of supervision are those that are important in therapy and counselling. Indeed, the supervisor has the chance to model these skills in the way in which he or she conducts the session. Overlapping skills include listening well, clarifying, encouraging the supervisee to express feelings, attending to counter-transference or congruence, working at the level of the supervisee, containing the supervisee's anxiety, creating safety through empathy and understanding, recognizing the dynamic in the relationship between supervisor and supervisee(s), perceiving links, remembering what appear to be keywords and phrases, as well as keeping to boundaries of time and role. Group supervision also needs group-facilitation skills.

But some of the skills are different, or less obviously used, in the practice of therapy. For example, there is a skill involved in acknowledging the line between colleague and supervisor – that the supervisor has a responsibility, and will need to challenge at times and sometimes more quickly and immediately than would be the case of a therapist who is trying to work with a client's defences; bad or risky practice needs to be faced straightaway, whatever the defences of the supervisee, although obviously the same skills involved in the therapeutic challenge are invaluable. A supervisor is probably more self-disclosing, encouraging a rather different sense of equality than would be usual between client and counsellor.

Then there is the fine line at times between attending to what has been stirred up in the supervisee by the work or by certain clients, so that the supervision is therapeutic as well as educative, but at the same time the supervisor should not actually slip into the role of therapist (see Question 4.3). Sometimes this means working with supervisees to see the parallels between their own life and the case they are working on, especially where there are difficult counter-transference feelings, but without this becoming therapy. Yet the supervisor also needs to be able to recognize when therapy would be of particular help to a supervisee and to point the supervisee in that direction without implying a sense of failure on the part of the supervisee.

Furthermore, where there is a dual role – supervisor as well as line manager (see Question 1.9) – this also requires the skill of being able to hold the different roles apart. At times, a supervisor, whether or not in a management role, will be compelled to be more judgemental and critical than would be the case in therapy, for example when there is obvious bad practice. Therapists who are unable to adapt their normal non-judgemental stance to the training or supervisory setting may not be able to be firm enough in the face of poor practice. Supervisors need the skill to recognize when someone is incompetent, as well as to demonstrate the necessary combination of confrontational and managerial skills to deal with such a situation.

There is also a different skill (although it is similarly present in brief therapy) of learning to work quickly, without harassing or hurrying the supervisee. The relatively short time for supervision compared to the work that a supervisee wishes to present means being even more alert to themes, transference, counter-transference, resistance and collusion, to possible parallel process (see Question 2.5) and to the focus of the supervisee's agenda. This means holding in mind a manageable agenda for each supervision session, as well as maintaining an overview of the supervisee's work. There is a particular skill in being able to carry through ideas from one supervision to the next so that they are not forgotten by the supervisee. The supervisor provides continuity for the presentation of the same case, as well as between cases.

A supervisor needs to educate and teach more than he or she would as a therapist, making concrete suggestions, helping to identify psychopathology and providing strategies, but also encouraging supervisees to reflect for themselves (see Question 3.5). This may also involve training supervisees to use supervision. Yet this agenda also needs to be able to provide space for supervisees to play creatively with ideas. Since the supervisor is training supervisees as part of their professional development, this means being able to identify training needs outside supervision and assisting the development of the counsellor's career. While supervisors have much to communicate, they also need to be wary of appearing all knowing, and need to contain their own not knowing as well as the anxiety of the supervisee at not knowing or not understanding. Good educators are also open to challenge, and so supervisors need to be able to take criticism from the supervisee and to allow for legitimate differences.

We are sure there are other skills we have not mentioned, indicating just how valuable it is to monitor one's work as a supervisor (see Question 3.6), since it is through feedback that these skills can be supported and strengthened. Handling the end of a supervision contract, or changes in pairings and groups, promoting anti-discriminatory practice, and not least being able to write clear and helpful reports (identifying strengths and weaknesses) are other skills that supervisors in training have identified as important to develop.

It is sometimes difficult to draw a precise line between skills and personal *qualities*, but we suggest that those qualities which have been identified as being essential in therapists are also essential in supervisors: the core conditions of empathy, congruence, acceptance, being comfortable with one's own authority and competence with appropriate self-disclosure, openness to not understanding, being able to be fallible and acknowledge mistakes, being patient, tolerant, calm and objective, flexible and clear-headed, together with a sense of humour are all important.

Finally, we believe there are certain *requirements* incumbent upon those who undertake the work of supervising others. They should certainly be experienced therapists or counsellors who are still in practice, even if their practice is not as large as it once was. It is so easy to forget just how difficult the practice of therapy and counselling is. We also think that a supervisor should keep a record of supervision sessions (see Question 3.4) and should be willing to fulfil the necessary administrative procedures that accompany supervising for agencies and courses. Finally, he or she should know when to seek her or his own supervision for the supervision he or she is offering when this is required (see Question 3.12).

* * *

3.2 I have been asked if I would like to supervise for a local voluntary counselling centre, and this will be my first experience as a supervisor. The centre wants me to see someone whom I know to be really experienced. Wouldn't it be better for me to see someone with little experience?

It is understandable, and probably indeed common practice, to match those who have no previous experience of supervision with those who have little or no experience of counselling. The assumption presumably is that the new supervisor will not be too taxed by the level of work and will be able to convey much basic knowledge and technique to the beginner, whose needs will be straightforward and simple. We have even come across examples where supervisors in training are used to supervise other students beginning their training as counsellors. It is difficult to understand how such policies can be justified, since trainee supervisors and novice counsellors all need to be learning in a secure environment, where they feel contained. Trying out new-found skills of supervision hardly provides the most stable environment for very inexperienced counsellors, and anxious new counsellors are hardly the most stable supervisees for supervisors to practise upon.

This type of matching is misplaced, and the assumption that accompanies it is wrong. Experienced supervisors know that their own therapeutic and supervisory skills are much more in evidence when working with experienced therapists than they are when working with those starting out in the profession. Experienced therapists have the ability to use their intuition, can play with material and have their own ideas as to what may be happening in the therapeutic relationship; all this helps to spark off the supervisor's own thinking so that supervision with experienced therapists becomes more like a dialogue between peers. But, unlike peer supervision, the supervisor can concentrate solely on the supervisee because the supervisor does not present her or his own work. Such supervision provokes much but actually demands little, since there is scant pressure to come up with answers, little need to check on the small but significant details of the therapeutic arrangements, less concern about technique and much more concentration upon the therapeutic relationship and its significance for understanding the client. This makes for a very good learning ground for the new supervisor.

Contrast this with working with novice counsellors. The material is generally less stimulating or, if it is stimulating, the supervisor has to hold in check her or his own bright ideas lest the supervisee feels undermined and ignorant. There are many basic issues that need to be overseen, if not through open questioning at least by careful listening. The didactic style of teaching features more prominently (see Question 3.5), and balancing such a style with the other skills of supervision is an added responsibility. Assessing standards is more difficult than when working with those who have proved their standards, and therefore help to create a benchmark for the supervisor, who then knows more clearly the goals which he or she wishes supervisees eventually to achieve. Issues of responsibility for the welfare of the clients are much more sharply defined when overseeing the work of new and nervous counsellors than when working with experienced therapists.

For these and other reasons, the offer that this questioner has been made is actually a good one. Anxieties about supervising well, about getting it right and about being able to make a fresh contribution are sure to be as present as they would be in working with an inexperienced supervisee, but these anxieties will be much better contained when working with someone who has a much clearer idea of what they should be doing. A supervisor's errors are unlikely to be acted upon by the experienced supervisee, who should be able to make an independent judgement about what can and cannot be applied back in the consulting room, and who uses supervision not to learn what to say and do but as a sounding board for her or his own exploration. New counsellors are prone to take as gospel what the supervisor says, even when it is not right, and to act upon it or even to misinterpret it. Supervisors have to choose their words much more carefully when working with impressionable beginners.

Although anxiety clearly lies behind the question, we wonder whether there might not be concern too about potential feelings of rivalry with a more experienced supervisee. How will the novice supervisor be regarded by the experienced supervisee? Surely, he or she will be critical of the other's ignorance or even of the supervisor's practice as a therapist (since this will be become more obvious in the interventions he or she makes)? How can an inexperienced supervisor tell an equal what to do? Such feelings are real enough, but they are again misplaced. If the supervisee is truly experienced as a therapist, he or she will not be looking for answers but for someone with whom he or she can share ideas, and for someone who understands how difficult it is to be certain of anything when working in such an intangible field. If the supervisee is truly mature, he or she will not be looking to score points, to undermine the supervisor or to rush to judgement. Supervision in such an instance should prove to be a very good situation in which to develop a new set of skills, while adapting other skills and knowledge to a fresh purpose.

* * *

3.3 I believe it is valuable to offer a contract to supervisees. What elements should I ensure are included in it?

Perhaps what is most important is ensuring that there is clarity on the basic boundaries of supervision. Contracts or agreements may be verbal or written but need to cover key areas, which both parties have discussed, negotiated and agreed. At the beginning of any new supervisory arrangement, there will be some sharing of basic information relating to the training, theoretical orientation, experience, previous supervision, work setting and caseload size of the supervisee, and the supervisor too will provide relevant information about their own background and experience, and ways of working in supervision. Similarly, some supervisees may work with children as well as adults, and the supervisor needs to be clear about whether or not they are qualified to do both. Whatever the preferences of both parties, it is important that there is a sufficient match in expectations and experience. Additionally, each should know the professional bodies to which the other belongs and to which code of ethics they subscribe.

If the contract is not a written one, it is none the less important to be sure the following areas have been discussed and agreed upon. We suggest that, if nothing else, it should be recorded and dated in the supervisor's notes that this has been done.

Payment

Cost is of obvious significance. How much a session costs, and whether it is for fifty or sixty minutes needs to be agreed – counsellors and therapists themselves vary in the length of therapy sessions offered; so supervisors cannot assume that their own sessions are standard and will be known and inherently agreed upon. Similarly, it is important to be clear if cancelled sessions are charged for, and at what point (for example charging if less than twenty-four hours' notice is given). Session fees are the most obvious cost, but, if supervisors are to be asked to write reports for courses or training bodies, they need to consider whether this cost is in their sessional fee or whether they require extra payment for the additional time involved.

If someone else is paying the supervisor (for example, an agency), both supervisor and supervisee need to know the procedure for claiming fees, who is to be invoiced and who is responsible if difficulties arise with payments. Although it may not be appropriate or possible to deal with this as part of the contract, difficulties can arise if payments from agencies are unreasonably delayed. We know of an instance where an irate supervisor threatened to withdraw supervision when six months of invoices remained unpaid. It is worth being aware that such issues around payment can powerfully affect the supervisory relationship.

Supervisors may well alter their fees at intervals. If costs are raised, supervisees need to be given sufficient warning and so a period of notice should also be agreed upon, for example three months' notice, for any increase. Some supervisors and therapists guarantee that their charges will remain static for a given period, such as one year.

Frequency

Frequency of supervision is the second aspect of a contract. This is potentially problematic if the supervisor thinks that what the supervisee requests is insufficient for their caseload and their level of experience. This should be negotiated so that supervisors do not take on a supervisee with whom they are uneasy. However, this is not always within the control of the supervisee, particularly if frequency of supervision is decided by a course or an agency and the supervisee is not in a position to afford more. Even where this is not the case, and frequency is mutually agreed, it is worth noting that circumstances can change for supervisees and may need to be reviewed. They may increase their workload or take on increasingly complex work, or work that is new to them. This points to the need for review (see below) at regular intervals.

Place and time

The place and time for supervisory sessions clearly need to be established. It is sometimes convenient and suitable to both for supervision to take place in the supervisee's home or workplace. This is especially likely if the supervisee has any difficulty with mobility, for example needing a wheelchair-accessible room, where the supervisor cannot provide this. If this involves the supervisor in travelling time, he or she needs to decide if this time is charged for. The venue should be suitable and preferably the same room at each meeting, although again this is not always possible if

supervising for agencies and courses. It is sometimes out of the control of
the supervisor and the supervisee: some aspects of the contract are dictat-
ed to rather than decided by the supervisory dyad. They nevertheless need
to be discussed. As with therapy itself, the room used should be quiet and
private, and the time should be uninterrupted. Mobile phones should be
turned off, and other interruptions should not occur (in an agency other
staff need to know that supervision as much as therapy is protected time
and must not be disturbed). As with therapy, if the supervisor is working
from home or private premises, supervisees need to know whether or not
there is a waiting room and whether or not they can arrive a few minutes
early, for instance to look at their notes, or whether they need to wait outside until their appointment. Sessions should begin and end on time.

Availability

Availability between sessions needs to be decided and clarified. If supervisees encounter particular difficulties between sessions, they need to
know whether they can ask for an extra session or can make telephone contact. Some supervisors charge for extra sessions but not for brief telephone
calls. In our experience, being available between sessions for supervisees
has never been misused and has on occasion been crucial for the therapy
as well as for the supervisee when a real difficulty has arisen. Clearly, if
there are frequent requests for extra sessions, this is likely to indicate that
meetings need to be more regular.

Process expectations

The above matters are all very significant and practical aspects of an agreement. However, exploring expectations of the actual process is similarly
significant. Supervisors may like supervisees to present in a certain way and
may have a preference for exploring one case in depth rather than many (see
Question 1.8). This may not match what the supervisee wants. Other supervisors think the supervisee should set the agenda and bring what he or she
wishes, presenting in a way that is comfortable to him or her. Some supervisors like working with tapes of sessions; others do not (see Question 1.11). If
tapes are used, it needs to be agreed whether they are listened to in the session or whether the supervisor will listen to a whole session beforehand:
there are obvious cost implications in this latter instance. Establishing the
limits of the supervisory process is necessary, for instance can the supervisee
bring organizational and other work issues or can they discuss a theoretical
paper with their supervisor, or is the focus to remain on client work?
   If supervisors expect supervisees to inform them of any specific situations, for example if a client is at risk or if there are child-protection issues,

this needs to be made clear. Supervisors working with independent practitioners will want to check that they are adequately insured and that suitable arrangements are in place in the event of serious and unexpected illness in the therapist, or even death, or of being unavailable for other reasons. Similarly, supervisors need to know if they are being asked to take on responsibility for informing clients in these circumstances, and they will then have to negotiate a mechanism for ensuring that they always have current contact information about the supervisee's clients. We address elsewhere the question of legal responsibility (Question 3.7); so accountability and the extent of confidentiality also need to be made clear. The supervisor may want to clarify what steps they would take if unhappy with the supervisee's practice.

Other supervisors

Some practitioners have more than one supervisor. This is particularly likely if they work in more than one context. They may have another individual supervisor or be part of a supervision group. While this need not be problematic, this needs acknowledging and exploring at the negotiation stage to identify the work that is to be brought to this supervision and to clarify the scope and purpose of any other supervision. This is especially important for beginning counsellors and therapists. Experienced practitioners are more likely to have developed a degree of clarity themselves regarding the roles of different supervisors and are more used to recognizing and defining their supervisory needs and expectations.

Context

Some aspects of contracting are context specific. If supervisors are employed by agencies or other organizations, they need be clear what is expected and whether or not this is acceptable to them. Agency expectations need to be transparent and any supervisory implications explored and agreed with the supervisee.

Reviews

Reviewing supervision, like the contract itself, may be formal or informal, verbal or written, but it is important to agree the frequency of reviews so that each has the opportunity to reflect on the process. Any dissatisfaction on either side can then be identified, acknowledged and discussed. This should be an open process, with both parties contributing equally to it. Agencies are likely to have their own review procedures in place, and at the contracting stage supervisors and supervisees should be made aware of these. Although urgent concerns should be addressed as they arise, a review provides an opportunity for reflecting on the total experience. It provides a place and time where either party can raise concerns about supervisory practice and style or the therapist's practice. Clearly, if there are major concerns about either of these, they should not be delayed for discussion until a review.

Dual relationships

Many supervisees and supervisors find themselves in dual relationships, that is they have some personal or professional contact outside the supervisory relationship. In many areas, this is unavoidable and has to be acknowledged and worked with. For example, many therapists and supervisors meet at professional meetings in their locality, and these meetings sometimes have a social as well as a professional aspect. Although it can be argued that the supervisory relationship should be kept pure and separate from other contexts, this is not always possible, and many people manage it very successfully. Although, as has been noted elsewhere, supervision can raise levels of anxiety and parental transferences (see Question 3.9) and some supervisees may try to use social contact to prevent too much attention to their work, for the most part, supervision is a working relationship between two adults. As such, it is reasonable to place some adult expectations on it, one of which is managing duality. Initial contracting provides the opportunity to explore any difficulties and dilemmas that may arise and to discuss ways for handling problems should they be identified.

It should be noted that no contract can anticipate every eventuality, and common sense has to prevail in these instances. A good rule of thumb is to expect the unexpected but to establish a culture of cooperation with the supervisee from the start, thereby developing the rapport that will enable any later difficulties to be explored and resolved.

* * *

3.4   Have you any advice on the best way of keeping track of the different clients my various supervisees present in supervision?

Supervisors have to retain the details of many more clients when they are supervising than they do when working as therapists. Remembering information from supervision sessions is indeed difficult, if not impossible, in any detail, because in supervision it is always second-hand, and therefore not so impressionable as when meeting people face to face. While larger issues, dramatic events and certain presenting problems may readily be recalled, losing the wider picture in supervision is not only a disadvantage but also a waste of time because the supervisee often has to remind the supervisor and others present when reintroducing a client who has been discussed before. Recording notes not only enhances supervision itself but also is essential should any concern or complaint about the supervisee ever occur.

We therefore have sought to develop a system whereby information can be recorded securely and in more detail than the often sketchy notes that supervisors make, but where there is also a fail-safe system of tracking the progress of supervisees and their clients, especially when there have been concerns either about the work of the supervisee or of the state of mind of the client. We recommend the following.

The supervisor's log

Although what we suggest can be written by hand in a notebook, and securely locked away for reasons of confidentiality between sessions, with the benefit of word processors it is possible to create a form of recording whereby each supervisee is allocated a file and where a running record can be kept of the clients they present. Such computer records do, of course, mean that the user has to be registered under the Data Protection Act (and ideally will be protected by a password), but, since client records may also be kept in that way by the therapist/supervisor, this small additional annual expense should not be an undue financial burden.

One possibility is therefore to record the individual supervisee in a file, such as Figure 3.1, where the clients are separately listed and notes are made for each client following a supervision session, but all within one supervisee's file. The fictitious supervisee in the example has a file that is divided into distinct parts for the fictitious clients recorded there. The advantage of this layout is that the sessions with the one client are in sequence, enabling an easier overview of the work. A second layout (Figure 3.2) records only by the supervisee's presentations, recorded session by session. In this layout, the supervisee has presented two clients in one supervision session. The third layout (Figure 3.3) can also be used in handwritten form and is the simplest form of log to write, although it is not necessarily the best form of log where there are a large number of supervisees and where it is the supervisor's practice to consult the record prior to the next supervision session. The overview of a client (Figure 3.1) or a previous session with that supervisee (Figure 3.2) is not so easily made.

Supervisee: *Joan Price*			date started supervision: 10.3.2002	
client: *TR*		1st session: 14.10.03	final session:	
date*	**no***	**material presented**	**issues considered**	
11.11.03	*3*	*confusing moving from work to family to psychosomatic symptoms*	*focus for counselling - need to identify link between the different topics*	
25.11.03	*5*	*settled to family issues - son and daughter not contacting him*	*whether can shift focus from what others done wrong to his guilt*	
13.1.04	*7*	*Missed sessions, particularly around Christmas break; pressures on JP in last session - 16.12.03 - to join in blame*	*perhaps feeling JP also pressuring to look at his responsibility. Discussed letter to TR to see if may return*	
client: *WT*		1st session: 7.1.04	final session:	
date*	**no***	**material presented**	**issues considered**	
13.1.04	*1*	*alcohol problems - anxiety when not drinking*	*motivation; anxieties about counselling; what if WT drinks before session?*	

*date means the date of the supervision session
*no. refers to the number of sessions the client has been seen

Figure 3.1 Recording by client and supervisee.

Supervisee: *Joan Price*			agency: *Binborough Coun Centre*
date	**client**	**material presented**	**issues considered**
13.1.04	*TR*	*Missed sessions, particularly around Christmas break; pressures on JP in last session - 16.12.03 - to join in blame*	*perhaps feeling JP also pressuring to look at his responsibility. Discussed letter to TR to see if may return*
13.1.04	*WT*	*alcohol problems - anxiety when not drinking*	*motivation; anxieties about counselling; what if WT drinks before session?*

Figure 3.2 Recording by supervisee.

These different types of form represent the record that the *supervisor* keeps, written up following each supervision session, although they are quite abbreviated. But there is a second form we have developed, which involves the supervisee as well as the supervisor.

date	supervisee	client	material presented	issues considered
13.1.04	J Price	TR	Missed sessions, particularly around Christmas break; pressures on JP in last session - 16.12.03 - to join in blame	perhaps feeling JP also pressuring to look at his responsibility. Discussed letter to TR to see if may return
13.1.04	J Price	WT	alcohol problems - anxiety when not drinking	motivation; anxieties about counselling; what if WT drinks before session?
20.1.04	B Lowe	Anne	reaction to impending finish	underlined need to work on ending which BL not good at

Figure 3.3 Recording by supervision.

The supervisee's record

This form (Figure 3.4 opposite) is one that every supervisee initially fills in before presenting any new client for supervision. On it, the supervisee includes some clear factual information together with a sketch of a number of features in the client's history. The supervisee completes the top row and the left-hand column, although the latter may be thin in some respects at the start or may have to be selective: if the client is brought to supervision after a single, initial counselling session, the amount of information may be very limited; if first brought to supervision some way into the counselling contract, there may be rather more information or so much that it needs to be kept to salient points. The notes supplied by the supervisee are in either case only a sketch.

This form is then handed to the supervisor – or, if there are other supervisees present, also copied for them, with each person writing their own name or initials into the 'supervisor' box. The form will be handed back to the person presenting at the end of the session for the supervisee to keep secure and, if the client is presented again, each of the others present receive back their initialled form, to continue adding their own notes to it. The supervisee is not expected to add anything more between times and, indeed, is not even obliged to read the notes. They are solely for the benefit of those supervising, whether as supervisor or co-supervisee(s). On their own forms they add anything else that emerges from the history, as subsequent sessions are reported. They also record in the right-hand column the date of the supervision session, the number of sessions or months to date the client has been seen and some brief remarks to act as an aide-memoire for themselves as to what they felt to be most significant in the presentation or in their own thinking. The aide-memoire is just that; it is not a note to the presenter to read later!

Client:	1st seen:	Contract		
Supervisor		**Presented for supervision**		
Presenting issues		date	sessions	supervisor's remarks
How relates in sessions				
Occupation				
Significant relationships				
mother				
father				
siblings				
partner(s)				
children				
others				
age	significant life events [d.o.b.]			

**This is confidential information – return this record to the supervisee
at the end of the supervision session.**

Figure 3.4 Client record form for supervision.

Although the form needs a little preparation before the first session and may need to be photocopied after the presenter has recorded the basic facts for presentation to any others in a supervision group, thereafter it represents very little work for those listening, who simply add occasional notes to it, as they themselves need to, and the record is kept secure between sessions in the supervisee's possession, because it is returned at the end of the presentation in the supervision session. Yet, for the little effort involved, it includes sufficient information for the client's story not to have to be repeated each time the client is presented and for the supervisor to track the progress of the work with the individual client.

* * *

3.5   Do I have a role as a teacher when I am a supervisor? Some of the inexperienced counsellors I supervise seem to need instruction as much as the opportunity to reflect on their work.

There is a fairly strong antipathy in the counselling philosophy to teaching – perhaps because it seems too much like giving advice, or it addresses head more than heart. Yet supervision is not identical to counselling and therapy, and one of the distinctions is that it gives more weight to elements that are more sparingly used, if at all, in the therapeutic relationship: to self-disclosure, advice and instruction. Carroll (1995), for example, lists seven tasks in supervision, including teaching and learning, evaluation and administration. Feasey is less keen on such 'schematic attempts at defining the role and tasks of the supervisor', preferring to place these different roles in a relational context (2002: 78). As a psychoanalytic psychotherapist, he is aware of the popular accusation that that approach often involves telling clients (and by implication supervisees) the meaning of their experience, which of course is very close to teaching, although Feasey eschews such a charge.

There is, in fact, a debate that runs through psychoanalysis (examined by Caligor, 1981) about the precise nature of teaching in supervision – is it analytic or didactic? The former implies the similarity between therapy and supervision; the latter stresses a more instructional role. The didactic approach is generally not as favoured, although it is recognized that supervision includes consideration of certain questions which may require some instruction. Anderson and McLaughlin in an early article, for example, suggest a teaching function, around assessment and establishing the right therapeutic atmosphere: how interpretation is most efficaciously used, how progress is judged and the interaction between theory and practice (1963: 78). They draw a distinction between the teaching of basic concepts, which will have taken place elsewhere in training, and the application of those concepts, and the rationale for using those concepts. They also assume that the supervisee has learned from her or his own personal therapy (1963: 83). Thus, supervision involves:

> . . . essentially a teaching process where certain elementary problems must be explored such as attitudes, procedure, activity, specific difficulties in getting an analysis underway and keeping it in progress, and supporting and directing a less experienced colleague until he develops sufficient understanding and confidence. The supervising analyst must believe in the value of teaching and of experience; he must not be too quick to fall back on the time-honored formula – 'you need more analysis'. (Anderson and McLaughlin, 1963: 93)

The last phrase is important. Is the supervisee's difficulty a personal one or is it simply that the supervisee has not yet been given sufficient opportunity to learn?

Typical of the other side of the debate are Fiscalini, whose phrase 'analysis by ventriloquism' is cited in several later articles that all draw attention to the danger of the didactic approach (1985: 602), and Frijling-Schreuder, who writes, 'For me the word "teaching" has connotations that are too intellectual and too authoritarian' (1970: 364; see also Question 2.9). Beiser's research (1982) into differences in the experience of supervision between child-analyst supervisors and non-child-analyst supervisors draws attention to aspects such as 'not actively managing the patient through the student', although also to phrases such as 'strong urge to be helpful' and 'enjoyment of teaching' (1982: 65), which may indicate a degree of didactic style. Perhaps child-analyst supervisors show less indication to teach because they are more used to playing as their main therapeutic approach, as in Aronson's useful description of teaching, which draws upon Winnicott's (1971) notion of the reliable, loving caretaker:

> As he [Winnicott] writes, 'responsible persons must be available when children play, but this does not mean that the responsible person need enter into the children's playing' ([1971] p. 50). This, to me, has ramifications for any teaching process. Supervisees need to discover who they are in relation to the 'not-me' of the supervisor, which is facilitated by the supervisor permitting this to occur by not impinging on the trainee ('lowering the degree of adaptation to the [supervisee's] needs'). A supervisor or teacher ideally delights in the student's magical discovery of material ('the capacity to find'). (Aronson, 2000: 125)

In a short but poignant article, albeit one that uses rather esoteric phrases, Levenson (1982) describes six categories of teaching supervision –

holding, Teutonic, algorithmic, metatherapeutic, Zen and preceptorship. He comes down on the side of the algorithmic method. In 'holding', the supervisor does very little, speaks rarely and allows the supervisee to explore with little interference. He describes his own supervision with Clara Thompson as an example: 'She didn't seem to want anything from us . . . she was like the Matterhorn – simply there' (Levenson, 1982: 4). The Teutonic method is like operating from a manual of prescribed situations and responses. Whatever is reported, the supervisor has an answer, which may make for a neat fit between theory and practice but is dismissed by Levenson as 'painting by numbers'.

The algorithmic method 'is designed so that one step leads to the other . . . [yet] the algorithm simply claims that if one follows the steps, the outcome results . . . . It may or may not have a theoretical idea behind it, but it makes no claim that the theory is necessarily related to the outcome' (1982: 5). The metatherapeutic approach sees supervision as an extension of the supervisee's therapy, with extensive use of the supervisee's countertransference. The Zen method refers to a supervisor who creates chaos: 'the supervisor harasses, raps, interferes until the therapist . . . lets go of all his preconceptions and tightness out of a sense of despair' (2002: 7). In preceptorship the supervisee learns from seeing what the supervisor makes of the same situation in a parallel process (see Question 2.5).

What emerges from this description of different styles of teaching is that they are, of course, also different styles of supervision. If we were therefore to turn this question a little on its head, and look to the supervisee's learning rather than the supervisor's teaching, we might suppose that learning comes from a variety of styles. It certainly comes from the supervisor modelling how therapy works – although the weakness of this as a sole method is that supervision and therapy are not identical, and what works in one (for example, rapid challenge in supervision when it is necessary) does not generally work well in the other. Learning comes from not knowing answers and the supervisor's encouraging the supervisee to play with and explore the issues. It comes from linking theory and practice, not as an intellectual game, but as extending the understanding and application of theory in relation to a particular client. It comes from being taught when a supervisee cannot reach a satisfactory answer – there are times when being didactic is helpful.

Like Feasey, we therefore see the teaching role as taking place within the context of a supervisory style that is relational and flexible. We value Winnicott's emphasis in the caretaker on adaptation. It may be necessary with inexperienced supervisees to instruct, briefly and to the point, especially when they just do not know what to do, or how to understand a situation. As supervisees advance in confidence in relation to practical skills, they may value allusions to theory that help them to make more sense of the client and of their own reactions. Supervisees can be encouraged to address questions themselves, with relevant information shared between supervisor and supervisee – each learning from the other. Such approaches are more consonant with a therapeutic style and reduce the power disparity between supervisor and supervisee (see Questions 2.9 and 3.9).

* * *

3.6 How might I monitor the effectiveness of my work as a supervisor?

We have indicated at several points in this book that the effectiveness of good supervision can be attributed to the same dynamic that can make therapy effective: that the presence of, the observations of and the relationship to another or others enable a person to reflect upon aspects of their thoughts, feelings, behaviours and relationships more objectively than is possible through subjective introspection alone. If this is true of therapy and supervision, it also implies that any monitoring of the supervisor also benefits from the observations of others.

In the answer to Question 3.12, we address one way of enabling this monitoring, that is supervision of the supervisor by an experienced colleague. We recommend reading that section of this chapter. In addition to that method of monitoring one's work, the most obvious people to provide feedback in a monitoring process are the supervisees themselves. Regular reviews (half-yearly for trainees, annually for those who are qualified) should be written into the contract made with supervisees, whether or not a training course or agency requires it (see Question 3.2). One part of the review (perhaps 60–70 per cent of the allocated time) concentrates upon the progress of the supervisee, but 30–40 per cent should be time for the supervisee to review the work of the supervisor.

There are, of course, difficulties inherent in such a review. Supervisees, especially if they are in training and their own review constitutes an important part of the assessment of their progress, may be reluctant to say anything that they fear might be critical of the supervisor. Our own experience in assessing supervisors, asking supervisees to comment upon specific skills that their supervisor has listed, is that they are 95–100 per cent supportive and rarely critical, even when the supervisor has made it clear that such critical attention is helpful and when we have ourselves, in our assessment of the same skills, remarked upon noticeable errors. This may often be because the errors we spot are generally failures to see possible parallels, to make links and to identify important issues. It may therefore be asking too much of supervisees to note similar omissions on the part of their supervisor, especially when they are seeking supervision to identify those aspects of their work that they have not themselves recognized as needing attention. Nevertheless, it is also our personal experience that constructive criticism from supervisees is more forthcoming when they are qualified therapists, where the question of their own assessment is not an issue and where a milieu of trust and openness has been created. Be wary of reviews that turn out to be completely positive!

For this monitoring, a checklist might be useful: it helps the supervisee know what he or she is meant to be commenting upon. Items from the lists of the knowledge, skills, qualities and requirements in good supervision in our answer to Question 3.1 might be included in such a checklist that asks for the supervisee's observations, whether written or verbal. For example, such a list might include the skills in Figure 3.5 opposite.

There is a less structured or less formalized way of receiving feedback from supervisors in the monitoring process. We have drawn attention, in the answer to Question 2.5 (p. 45), to Langs' (1979) comment that the supervisor should listen to the client's communication, as reported by the supervisee, as firstly referring to the supervisor, or to the supervisory relationship. Thus, when the client is reported as saying 'I felt bruised last week', this may be a reference to the supervisee's feeling bruised by the forceful manner of the supervisor (the example comes from Jones, 1989). Such an interpretation does not deny that the client used those words, but asks why those words were selected by the supervisee for emphasis in reporting. We think that the supervisee's own remarks about the client also need to be heard as potentially referring to the supervisor. Such a proposal draws upon the psychodynamic idea of displacement, or 'unconscious communication' (Langs, 1979), where what is said about other situations outside the face-to-face relationship possibly refers as well to the present, here-and-now situation. Unlike Langs, we would not press such an interpretation at every opportunity, but we do suggest that, as in therapy itself, a supervisor needs to be watching and listening for reactions to her or his interventions and style of supervision. For example, a supervisor notes that the supervisee seems rather hot and bothered and so interrupts the presentation: 'You appear rather anxious today.' 'Yes,' replies the supervisee. 'I felt I received quite a lot of stick last time for my presentation, and I want to get it right today.' This observation of non-verbal communication (like Jones' example above of the unconscious communication in 'I felt bruised last week') allows for the type of ongoing monitoring that is the ideal of all good therapy and supervision. While it may be that the supervisee needs some correction, the supervisor can at this point reflect upon whether her or his critical tone is too strong and whether a more sensitive approach to challenge is necessary, either overall or with this particular supervisee.

The third way of monitoring (apart from the use of an external supervisor) is the use of taping. We address some issues around taping in

Empathic communication with therapist and about client(s)
Clarity of communication with therapist
Match of theoretical ideas with therapist's understanding
Ability to give supportive feedback
Style of critical responses to therapist's work
Facilitation of open/honest dialogue in supervision
Understanding of counsellor's setting/agency
Sensitivity to personal issues in the therapist
Reliability – times, dates, remembering clients

Figure 3.5 Example of a review checklist for monitoring supervision.

Question 1.11, and some of the caution we express there applies in supervision too. Permission to tape must be sought, and freely given, and confidentiality about clients must be assured. Generally, this is less troubling and less intrusive for supervisees than it can be for some clients. Reflective listening to such a tape, like other methods of review, can be very revealing. We often see, after the event and at a distance from it, what we did not spot or did not stop ourselves saying at the time.

Even better, it may be possible to use a tape of supervision with another experienced supervisor, who can listen to it at a convenient time and then comment upon it in person. Taping is a method we use in the assessment of supervisors in training, and we are convinced that detailed analysis, even if only on one session or part of a session, is the richest of all learning experiences. It is, of course, time-consuming, and a transcript is sometimes necessary when using the tape with another, but the effort involved is repaid tenfold, with the amount of comment, both supportive of fine interventions and observant of errors and omissions, very considerable.

* * *

3.7   How far am I responsible for the work of my supervisees? Suppose a complaint is made against one of them by a client: could I be held responsible too?

For the fullest answer to this important question, and other matters of law that might arise in and through supervision, we recommend consulting the companion volume in this series on questions of law (Jenkins et al., 2004), where there are frequent references to this aspect of therapeutic practice. In respect of this particular question, Jenkins et al.'s answer to a very similar question (2004: Question 6.5) is particularly relevant. We summarize their answer here, although urge consulting the full version in their book since, as they write, 'the role of the supervisor . . . does have potential legal ramifications' (2004: 99). We also suggest other references at the end of this answer.

Because issues may arise where a counsellor has a troubled and troublesome client, which may or may not be a situation exacerbated by the responses the counsellor is making to that client, supervisors need from the outset to clarify and agree exactly how much the supervisor is responsible for, how much any agency or organization where the counsellor may be working holds responsibility and how much devolves upon the shoulders of the supervisor. This is part of the contract (see Question 3.3). There may also be a contract between the supervisor and an agency, an employing organization or a training course, which includes a clause about reporting concerns about clients or questionable practice.

Although many supervisors assume clinical responsibility for the work of their supervisee(s), Jenkins et al. observe that the term 'clinical responsibility' is rather loaded, since it introduces, but does not clearly resolve, just how much a supervisor is actually responsible, in a legal sense, for the mistakes and practice of the supervisee. There may also be differences here between the law as it is applied in the United Kingdom, and elsewhere. In the United States, for example, supervisors have been held liable for their supervisees' practice.

We need to remember that, while a counsellor may have regular supervision, supervisors do not have a detailed knowledge of the clients being seen, and they may have no direct connection with an agency, organization or training course. As Jenkins et al. observe, 'much counselling and psychotherapy supervision is carried out "at arm's length"' (2004: 101). How can a supervisor be held legally responsible when a therapist may not disclose mistakes or paints an inadequate picture of the risks involved in working with a particular client? We have ourselves (in Question 1.1) defined supervision as partly involving much that is not known. Supervision for counsellors and therapists is more a form of professional consultation than line management (see Question 1.9), although the two roles are often confused in the case of similar professions such as social work and nursing.

Jenkins et al. suggest that 'whether or not the supervisor is liable for the work of their supervisee, and therefore could be sued, depends critically on the existence of a duty of care' (2004: 101). If the law held that there was no duty of care in supervision, it would be unlikely that a supervisor could be sued for damages. The contract for supervision is between the counsellor and supervisor, and the client is not a party to the contract so cannot therefore sue the supervisor (under a defence called 'privity of contract'). Given that they probably cannot sue the supervisor either under negligence law as a third party (unless they sue the employing organization, like an NHS Trust), their only recourse against the supervisor is probably via a complaint to the supervisor's professional association. A supervisor does, however, owe a duty of care to the therapist and should therefore work to ensure at least the minimum standards of competency in the supervisee, as well as demonstrate competency as a supervisor (see Question 3.1). A therapist, in theory at least, could sue the supervisor for breach of this duty of care.

And might a supervisor also owe a separate duty of care to the client? Jenkins et al. raise that question too: 'In other words, could the *client* sue the *supervisor* for failing to spot the therapist's ineffective, damaging or abusive work? To be honest, the answer to this question is not clear, and there are differing points of view on this between the authors themselves, as there are amongst other writers on this topic' (2004: 101, italics in the original). There are counter-arguments to Jenkins et al.'s position about the limited extent of supervisor responsibility in law in Griffin (2001: 8–9) and Leonard and Richards (2001: 192–197).

One view is that it might be held that the professional relationship between supervisee and supervisor is sufficiently close that the supervisor *should* have a detailed knowledge of the therapy and should therefore be able to stop the client coming to harm. This is a possibility, although it is also speculation. Another angle involves the relationship between supervisor and supervisee in relation to employment – are both employed by the same organization? Jenkins et al. give a possible example, where 'a client with a grievance against a psychotherapist in the NHS . . . would sue the NHS Trust, which employed that therapist. If the supervisor was also employed by the same NHS Trust, the Trust would also be vicariously liable for any inadequate supervision' (2004: 102). But they also point out that 'the concept of vicarious liability offers an umbrella of protection to therapists and supervisors, in that the employing organization is in the immediate line of fire, and can provide legal representation for them' (2004: 102). Yet, to complicate the speculation even further, 'the same employer is also at liberty to bring later disciplinary proceedings against the staff concerned, should there have been a major breach of accepted policy and practice, such as, for example, a failure to report a child at clear risk of abuse' (2004: 102).

At the core of this legal speculation lies the question of the nature of the supervisor's relationship to the supervisee and agency concerned. Most supervisors are not directly employed by an organization, partly for reasons of separating supervision and line management (see Question 1.9). In these, the majority of cases, according to a strict reading of employment law, the supervisor does not carry vicarious liability for the counsellor.

Jenkins et al. remind us that 'the issue of supervisor liability, in a narrow legal sense, has yet to be resolved by case law' (2004: 102). They also underline the importance of supervisors being adequately covered by professional indemnity insurance as supervisors, not just as therapists, just in case.

There is one further aspect to this question, which does not involve the law but is nevertheless of possible concern to the questioner. If a complaint is made against a supervisee, that complaint is likely to be made first to the supervisee and, failing resolution, to the supervisee's professional organization. In the course of our work, we have heard of too many examples where, in the initial stages, supervisors have supported the counsellor against the complainant, by pathologizing the client and insisting the supervisee stands firm against what is sometimes described by the supervisor as manipulative behaviour on the part of the client. Instead, had the supervisor looked at what substance there was in the complaint, at what other factors might have given rise to it, and had helped the supervisee to handle it in order to give the complainant a voice, we believe that some complaints would have gone no further. There is a useful section in the BACP's 'Ethical Framework' (2002: 8) headed 'If things go wrong with own clients', which merits study by supervisors as well, as it provides sound guidance on the steps that should be taken when there is a complaint, or the possibility of a complaint, in order both to acknowledge the possible hurt and to prevent the complaint going further than it need to. The supervisor can thus help supervisees in trying to resolve any conflict with a client and, if necessary, might want to advise their supervisees to make use of an independent means of mediation, such as a client or consumer advocacy service (e.g. UK Advocacy Network).

If it does go further, and the client is not satisfied or cannot be satisfied, a supervisor may be called upon to act as a support person, a 'friend' to the supervisee at a professional adjudication or tribunal. The supervisor's ability to support the supervisee in this process is very important, since it is a highly troubling procedure for both complainant and therapist to go through. A supervisor may also be able to provide chapter and verse in written or oral submissions about the presentation of the client in question in supervision, demonstrating where the counsellor has acted responsibly by discussing matters in supervision. Such detailed evidence of supervision, where it took place, is of far greater importance than generalized references, which may praise a counsellor's work generally but fail to comment on the particular issue.

For assisting in matters of complaints and professional bodies, we recommend Casemore (2001) – see also Daniels (2000) and Jenkins (2001: 22–40).

* * *

3.8 I have just been asked to be an external supervisor for a student on a training course. What might this involve, and what do I need to ensure is in place to undertake this task properly?

Supervising a student on a course is invariably somewhat different from supervising in other contexts. It is likely that the supervisor will be involved in the assessment process, and it is also likely that the supervisee is relatively inexperienced, unless they are in advanced training, of course. If this is the first stage of training, the supervisor has to be prepared for the supervisee's being unused to the process and potentially anxious about both supervision and the course.

Perhaps the first question supervisors need to ask themselves is whether or not they are happy to supervise trainees on a particular course. If the course is BACP accredited, some assumptions can safely be made. The supervisor can be assured that the course has gone through rigorous procedures and that the student-selection process, the course's content, procedures, supervision requirements, quality of teaching staff and other resources will have been closely monitored. This does not mean that a course that is not accredited is not satisfactory: it may be too new to have yet gone through the necessary procedures or may not fit the criteria in some way, yet it can still be competent and professional in its approach. Courses often acquire a reputation for good or ill in the immediate locality, and so, if in doubt, it may be wise to ask around.

However, it is worth asking more robust questions of a course that has not been vetted by an external and thoroughly reputable organization. It is worth bearing in mind that some organizations sound impressive but have less actual substance. As a rule of thumb, courses that do not welcome external supervisors asking questions or do not respond adequately might be better avoided.

Given this initial aspect of course credibility, there are other areas to consider. Assessment has already been referred to, but it is extremely important to be clear about the supervisor's role in this. Does the supervisor know what he or she is being asked to do and when to do it? Is he or she able and willing to fulfil such requirements? Does the supervisee know about the assessment, and is there a transparency in the process? If the supervisor is to be involved in assessment, both supervisor and supervisee need to know the parameters of this from the beginning of their work together, exploring how it might affect it. It is also necessary to know what form the assessment takes, for instance does it involve completing a form or writing a report with or without guidelines? Is the report written individually and independently or is the process a mutual one, undertaken jointly with the supervisee, with the supervisor also being subject to assessment? This can involve considerable time, and it is therefore important to ascertain who pays for this time. What importance and weight are given to the assessment? For example, does the supervisor have to state that the student has reached a pass standard on their counselling work? If this is the case, what criteria are to be used in reaching this decision?

If the supervisor does not feel the supervisee has reached the required standard, what happens then? Many courses will not allow a student to progress without reaching a satisfactory counselling standard as decided by the supervisor, although we have known others where a supervisor failing a student has had the decision inappropriately over-ruled. And, if the supervisor is not part of the assessment process and does not feel the student's standard is good enough, what mechanisms are in place for this to be communicated to the course? A supervisor needs to be confident that her or his voice will be heard and taken seriously if there are concerns. It will also be necessary to check on whether assessment is only at the year's end or whether there is a midway point in the year, where both the student and the course can be alerted to any difficulties that may prevent the student from passing. If this is not in place, it is worth suggesting it or making such an interim formative assessment independently. It is also necessary to know if the student has another supervisor and, if so, how the role is to be shared. If it is, what are the respective responsibilities? And how can it be ensured that this is a positive experience for the student and that unhelpful splitting does not take place?

Courses need to consider worst-case scenarios and have clear procedures in place if they occur in clinical practice, especially when external supervision is used. If supervision is 'in house', with supervisors forming a direct part of the course team, difficulties can more easily be recognized and responded to. Communication is easier and there is a natural meeting point for the team. This is not the case for independent supervisors. While the contribution of the independent supervisor is crucial, it may not always feel that way. Courses need to send out accurate information before the process starts. This should include clear details of what to do and who to contact if there is any concern about the student's work. There is a major issue about who is responsible if concerns arise, so this needs to be clarified.

There is another aspect that involves a potentially problematic triangular situation. A supervisor may not be dissatisfied with the work of the student as such but may feel concerned that her or his placement is unsuitable. This is most likely to occur in areas where placements are at a premium and courses are anxious to take students to fill places, even when insufficient suitable placements are available. This can lead to a lack of rigour and, for example, to students with little or no mental-health experience or knowledge working with very disturbed clients. They can be counselling in settings where there is little support and where there is no prior assessment by an experienced practitioner of the client's suitability for counselling, especially that which is offered by trainees. Insufficient knowledge and experience, rather than inherent unsuitability, can lead to trainees being completely out of their depth. This is worrying for supervisors, who may find themselves trying to contain and manage the work and its impact in a context where they have no control over the placement and yet are fully involved in trying to resolve the resulting difficulties.

As well as being satisfied that the course is of a sufficient standard and what is required of supervision, the same is true of a placement: the relationship with the placement provider is another area to be considered. This would also be the case if supervisees are not trainees, but it has a particular resonance and gives rise to particular responsibilities when they are. It is important to ascertain that both the course and the placement think that the supervisor is appropriate to the supervisee, and clearly supervisors themselves need to feel sure of this. Some courses build in the possibility of a three-way meeting for the course, the placement and supervisor if there are any difficulties; some give such communication priority and ensure contact is clearly built into the course structure, but some do not appear to show any concern for this dimension.

Another issue is that while many courses restrict new trainees from undertaking private practice in order to get experience others do not.

Supervisors may find themselves deeply concerned that inexperienced practitioners are working in private practice without the necessary skill and experience base to support such work. This can be avoided by early discussions with the course. The course has the primary responsibility for ensuring both that great care is taken over these issues and that potential supervisors are given accurate and full information before they commit themselves to working with the supervisee.

It is important to remember that a request for supervision can be turned down if it is not considered that the course or the student is of a good enough standard. Supervisors should be expected to have worked out what they need in place to supervise competently and professionally and to hold their own authority. Supervising a student who is competent, communicative and responsive and who uses supervision well, as often comes from supervising trainees, can be an extremely enjoyable experience for both parties. Supervising someone who is learning fast, who is enthusiastic about their training and who is on a good course that can be respected and trusted enables a supervisor to make a positive contribution to the profession, as well as to the student. However, because these arrangements do not always go well and supervision can give rise to some deep concerns, close attention to the aspects outlined here is crucial.

* * *

3.9   I have to present a report at the end of the year on supervisees from a particular course as part of their assessment. Surely, the fact they know this will make it much more difficult for them to be really honest about their work with me, especially if they say or do something that is bad practice?

Although it is impossible ever to know how honest anyone is without external evidence to verify their statements, to acknowledge that supervisees in training are probably concerned about assessment, as well as that supervisees are generally concerned about criticism, means that a supervisor is halfway towards working with this particular difficulty. The anxiety that supervision gives rise to is well documented, and in our answer we summarize some of the thinking around the causes of that anxiety. If the anxiety can be addressed, the hope must be that a supervisee can be more open about her or his work. One of us recalls an experienced therapist once saying that there was something she wanted to talk about, which she could not take to her other supervisor, although it belonged to that setting. Why she was unable to share certain things was not explored in our session, since that was a matter for her and her supervisor. But it appeared that the anxiety was less with one supervisor than it was with another.

A study of the factors that might block openness on the part of supervisees is reported by Webb and Wheeler (Webb and Wheeler, 1998; Webb, 2000). Half of the sample group of supervisees were in training. The study can be summarized as identifying five features that influenced the degree of openness, which we take to be similar to the honesty that is referred to in this question:

1. Supervisees in individual supervision were more likely to disclose sensitive issues than those in group supervision.
2. The degree of rapport between supervisor and supervisee influenced the degree of openness.
3. Supervisees in training were significantly less able to disclose sensitive issues.
4. Supervisees supervised outside their own work setting were significantly more able to disclose sensitive issues than those who were supervised within their work setting; this included openness not only about clients but also about supervision itself.
5. Supervisees who had chosen their own supervisor were significantly more able to disclose sensitive issues than those who had been allocated a supervisor. (See Webb, 2000: 64–65)

While this study presents a snapshot of comparative openness in different supervisory settings, the question remains about what it is that may create anxiety or enable trust. One of us can think of a situation where an experienced therapist, with generally good rapport, supervised outside his setting, in individual supervision with a supervisor he had chosen, was still unable to reveal a very troubling relationship with a client. No one is exempt from the difficulty.

There are some helpful indicators in a number of sources as to what might make honesty difficult. For example, supervision involves the discussion of issues that can be active in the supervisee as well as in the client. Hartung (1979) suggests that learning, such as takes place in supervision, involves entering what he calls the latency mode, but, whereas much of the learning outside the field of therapy and counselling is around topics that can be discussed without directly impinging upon the emotions of the learner, supervision involves the discussion of emotions with which the supervisee may not feel altogether comfortable. It can therefore be hard to be explicit about what a client describes, or what the supervisee experiences in the transference and counter-transference, without feeling stimulated by those feelings, which can lead in turn to shame or guilt and the need to hide or disguise them.

Supervision involves being attached to competent people, in order to learn from them, but such a state also means being 'relatively free of the continual stimulation of oedipal and preoedipal themes in order for energy to be available to put into the task of learning' (Hartung, 1979: 47). Overstimulation of feelings towards a supervisor may therefore inhibit the learning situation, since he or she is confused with other significant people in the supervisee's experience. Instead of there being a working relationship between supervisor and supervisee, therefore, the supervisee transfers unresolved issues, restimulated either by the supervisory relationship or by the material brought to supervision. For example, a supervisee may not be able to share material because the supervisor is seen as a parental figure, perceived perhaps as authoritarian (see Question 2.9), seductive or inhibiting. Searles (1962: 585) points to the tendency of some students to see the supervisor either as the feared, hated or despised super-ego or the opposite: the ego-ideal, oracular, with all the student's best capacities given to the supervisor. Hartung (1979) adds that learning, including supervision, may raise separation/individuation issues: the supervisee in training is put in the position of doing what parental figures require, giving rise to the fear of loss of individuality. Kadushin (1968) similarly writes that supervision involves change, the critical examination of ideas and practice even of one's own personality, giving up old patterns, giving up independence and autonomy to depend upon the teacher, submitting to authority and sharing one's ignorance. There is always the risk of criticism, shame or even rejection. Like the other sources referred to here, Kadushin says that supervision reactivates old parent–child relationships.

Rivalry often makes it difficult to work in group supervision, since admitting certain feelings or mistakes may be seen as falling below the others, but there may also be competition in individual supervision with the supervisor. Hartung observes that this may partly involve the difficulty in surpassing one's teacher because of the fear of doing better than the parent or teacher, and Searles makes a point about competition (1962, 601–602; see also Question 2.4) that it is difficult to share compassionate feelings and so intellectual competitiveness takes their place. While not altogether an explanation of the anxiety that a supervisee may experience, both those sources imply that in rivalrous situations it may be more difficult to admit shortcomings, for fear of giving the other the upper edge.

Among the feelings that it may be more difficult to own are negative feelings about clients – although supervisors recognize how useful it is to share such reactions, since counter-transference feelings can inform the work. Robinson (1949), writing from a social-work perspective, describes a persistent and fundamental tendency in the natural helper to deny negative aspects of feeling and to try again and again to build wholes that exclude those aspects: 'Those who choose social work as a profession have long since, probably in their earliest relationship, identified the self with goodness, and want to do good to the other. No theoretical teaching about ambivalence touches this fundamental organization of the self, but it must be touched if it is to deal with the reality of human "badness" as it needs to be expressed by the client' (1949: 63–64). Robinson (1949) quotes Jessie Taft:

> The price one pays for success in denying negative feelings is a lessening of the ability to feel positively. Feeling is one. It goes with whatever the self admits is vitally important. To be able to feel, one must be willing to care. And to care is to expose one's self to loss or injury or defeat as well as to fulfilment and success.
>
> The goodness or badness of an emotion is determined, then, not by pleasantness or unpleasantness, not by its positive or negative, uniting or separating character, but by the extent to which the individual accepts it as a part of himself, a necessary reflection of his own evaluation of living, instead of projecting it completely upon an external cause. (Robinson, 1949: 68)

A variation on a similar aspect is identified by Mollon (1989), when he describes how inexperienced therapists 'can experience turmoil when the patient is hostile, rejects what is offered and attacks the therapist's professional identity' (1989: 113). As Robinson points to the positive feelings a practitioner believes he or she should have, so Mollon points to the positive feelings that an inexperienced therapist believes clients will have towards them. Sharing those feelings in supervision may therefore raise anxiety, since the supervisee is experiencing what Mollon calls 'narcissistic perils' (1989: 113). This antipathy on the part of the client may include what Searles suggests is criticism for not being made well, and he observes that a supervisee can get caught between the client's intense criticism on the one hand and the supervisor's disapproval on the other (1962: 587; see also Question 2.4). Where the supervisee's self-esteem is at risk, openness may not appear to be the best policy.

Although there must also be other causes for the anxiety that inhibits honesty in supervision, we must not forget the one identified by the questioner – that assessment lies round the corner. Training for a qualification means being careful about appearing competent. Ironically, supervisors know that honest incompetence, at least on an occasional basis, is better than dishonest competence. But how far dare a supervisee own errors and omissions before the axe comes down?

Loss of self-esteem, which appears to be the most powerful constraint on honesty, is also suggested by Kadushin as the motivating factor behind what he describes as the games that supervisees play. Writing from both a social-work and a transactional-analysis perspective, he identifies a keen desire on the part of the supervisee to keep losses to a minimum and to maximize the rewards from supervision. In order to do this, supervisees can play games of one sort or another.

Kadushin's descriptions are somewhat tongue in cheek, yet they point to ways in which supervisees may use certain tactics to avoid having to speak fully and openly about their therapeutic work. They may therefore try to hook the supervisor into a joint moan about the agency, form-filling, etc. He calls this 'Two against the agency'. They may seek to flatter the supervisor, in order to distract her or him from looking more deeply at the detail ('Be nice to me because I am nice to you'). They may try to redefine the relationship by playing on the ambiguity of the roles in supervision. The supervisee may therefore expose her or his own difficulties rather than those arising in the work ('Protect the sick and infirm' or 'Treat me don't beat me'), trying to turn supervision into therapy (see Question 4.3) or trying to lessen the scrutiny of supervision by emphasizing the friendly side of the relationship – and putting off the hard work that is to be done.

Intellectualization can be a way to distract the supervisory session away from the expression of feelings that are thought to be inappropriate or from a closer examination of the therapeutic relationship. This is one of Kadushin's most amusing examples. He calls the game 'If you knew Dostoevsky like I know Dostoevsky'. During supervision, the supervisee makes a casual allusion to the fact that, for example, 'the client's behaviour reminds me of that of Raskolnikov in *Crime and Punishment*, which is, after all, somewhat different in aetiology from the pathology that plagued Prince Myshkin in *The Idiot*'. Such phrases can be followed up with 'You do remember, don't you?'. Other diversionary tactics include suggesting the supervisor does not understand the setting, concentrating on external social factors, only relating the client's history and not sharing any of the 'give-and-take' of the counselling session itself, being very selective about what he or she presents, sharing without affect or overwhelming the supervisor with trivia ('What you don't know won't hurt me'). Any of these ploys can prevent a full examination of the material and particularly of the supervisee's interventions.

Kadushin further identifies the problem that is inherent in encouraging supervisees to set the agenda; in this way they may present only cases where things are going reasonably well and not report on those that are not. Or the supervisee brings a series of questions about her or his work that need to be discussed, which sends the supervisor off into mini-lectures and takes the heat off the supervisee ('I have a little list'). Variations on this include 'Little old me' or 'Casework à trois', where the supervisee unloads responsibility onto the supervisor, or a further instalment of this where the supervisee applies the supervisor's prescriptions 'in spiteful obedience' and acts as though the supervisor were responsible for the case and as if the student is just the executor of supervisory directives ('I did like you told me'). Since the supervisor shares some responsibility for the case, the supervisor can hook into this and enjoy acting the capable parent to the dependent child.

Somewhat different in the list of games (and there are others Kadushin lists) is 'Heading them off at the pass', because here, as opposed to hiding the true nature of the work, the supervisee freely admits her or his mistakes because he or she knows that he or she has done badly but is so self-flagellating that the supervisor has little option but to reassure and be sympathetic. This subtly prevents any real work being done.

All these games are, of course, caricatures, but there is some truth in them. They highlight and occasionally exaggerate some selective but essentially truthful aspects of the supervisory relationship. What is ignored in all this is that it is not only supervisees who feel anxious. Supervisors do, too, and may therefore act in ways that inhibit the honesty of their supervisees. Kadushin identifies just two games that supervisors play, although Hawthorne (1975) has responded to Kadushin's emphasis on the supervisee by listing others that involve supervisors. Where a supervisor plays intellectual games, parades knowledge or has an answer to everything, it will not be surprising that supervisees react either by trying to match such tactics or by hiding their own ignorance. Where a supervisor is hypercritical, only correcting and seldom supporting, honesty may not seem to be the best policy.

* * *

3.10 I work full time as a therapist and am building up a supervision practice. I am very clear about how many clients I take on, but how might I decide how many supervisees?

It is good for the professional development of a therapist to engage in a variety of tasks, even if they all are related to the one discipline. To be able to supervise counsellors and therapists, and to use the experience gained in this way, is not only rewarding – it makes for a sufficiently different way of working to ring the changes in the daily round. It is vital that a supervisor is still in practice, and this questioner clearly is. There is no suggestion here of exchanging a therapy practice for supervision.

While it is impossible to set down a formula for the best proportion of clients to supervisees, the factors that make for such a decision can be outlined. First of all, a supervisor has to hold many more clients in mind than the number of supervisees. Seeing just two supervisees who see two clients each makes four people in all who are to be contained in supervision. Methods of recording, in order to aid memory and prevent too much recapping each time are outlined in the answer to Question 3.4. But, clearly, seeing too many supervisees also means having to juggle much more information, and this might not be helpful either to the supervisees or to their clients. Supervision involves a considerable amount of thoughtfulness, and thinking about too many clients in a relatively short time can be more tiring than practising therapy. Not only do supervisees need space to reflect: a supervisor also needs mental space to be able to give sufficient attention to each client presented.

A second factor is the amount of paperwork necessary outside supervision. Unlike the work with clients, reports on supervisees are generally going to be necessary in one form or another: supervisees in training will probably need assessment; supervisees who are working in agencies may need annual appraisal. Notes need to be made regularly, not only to refer back to but also in case of any later query. While none of this need be overwhelming, it is another drain on time, often in addition to the pattern of appointments each week.

There may be other considerations, for example supervisees, while representing a more reliable commitment than some clients (who may not always see out a contract), also make for a more definite contract. Clients come and go, and adjustments to the number of clients can therefore be made more easily; spaces do not have to be filled if there are other pressures. Supervisees are likely to be around for longer, although they may be more adaptable in being able to change times when necessary. Taking on a new supervisee is like taking on a long-term client. This may again influence the proportion of counselling and supervision that the practitioner wishes to plan.

* * *

3.11 What is the ideal size for group supervision?

As the answer to Question 4.7 suggests, five or six supervisees makes for an ideal number in a group since, in a weekly group meeting of 90 minutes, this permits each person to present fairly frequently (if two people take half the time each, they are able to present every three weeks). The other important factor is that this number enables a number of different methods of supervision to be used – again see Question 4.7 – whereas too few (especially when one person is absent) scarcely makes a group, and too many makes for less participation.

There are other considerations that dictate group size. There needs to be a large enough room, with comfortable seating and, given the variety of methods we suggest in Question 4.7, space to move chairs when necessary. The needs of the supervisees for a specified amount of supervision time each month, which some organizations such as BACP require for continuing accreditation status, also means that the size of the group dictates how much additional supervision its members may require. For a calculation of this, see the second part of the answer to Question 2.8.

* * *

3.12 How much supervision of my supervision work should I have? And is this really necessary? Who supervises the supervisors of supervision?

As we indicate in a number of answers to other questions, the value of another's perspective is one of the essential components of therapy, and this applies equally to supervision. It is therefore clear that to be supervised upon supervision work also has benefits, although we are also bound to say that there must be a law of diminishing returns: while the emotional distance of the supervisor is a benefit (Searles, 1962: 587), the farther away the process gets from the original interaction, the less sharp is the focus. So for the supervisor of supervision also to have supervision does seem reminiscent of those endless cause-and-effect arguments for the existence of God (Jacobs, 2000: 201)!

Such a *reductio ad absurdum* does not diminish the value of the experience of supervision of a supervisory practice. We have always required it when training supervisors, though not at the same intensity as counsellors and therapists receive supervision. It may be that the supervisor of a therapist's work can occasionally assist with that therapist's supervisory practice, as long as this is agreed in the contract between supervisor and therapist as being on the agenda – either in occasional additional sessions or using part of normal supervisory hours. The use of tapes of supervisory sessions is addressed in the answer to Question 3.6, where we underline how much there is to be learned from monitoring supervision work (see also Question 3.1, where the training for supervisors is supported). If there is occasion in a supervisory practice to need an external opinion (for example, where there are possible ethical or legal issues), here again consultancy is recommended.

A number of writers on supervision agree that the time has come in the development of counselling in the United Kingdom to wonder whether the regulation of supervision in some quarters is really necessary for experienced practitioners (Jacobs, 2000: 201–202; Shipton, 2000: 203–204; Wheeler, 2000: 204–206). They argue that too much regulation on supervision erodes the principle of self-regulation, self-monitoring and self-responsibility. For this reason, while we support the training of supervisors and the supervision of supervision on an occasional basis, as well as supervision when particular difficulties arise with a supervisee's work, we believe, along with some other professional groups, that experienced practitioners should be trusted to monitor their work, whether it is through training, supervision or in their therapy practice, knowing for themselves at what point to take steps, both when they are aware that another's assistance is necessary and understand the benefits of another's view.

CHAPTER 4

The supervisor: further issues

4.1 I am very concerned about the practice of one of my supervisees. What is the best way of tackling this?

Hopefully, in the initial contracting or agreement with this supervisee (see Question 3.3 about contracts) there was discussion of what steps might be taken if there was dissatisfaction on either side of the supervisory dyad. Dissatisfaction with a supervisor is raised in Question 2.9; here we are concerned with dissatisfaction with a supervisee.

A supervisor may be unhappy with all of the work being presented or with just one case; he or she may have always been uneasy about the work or something may have changed giving rise to more recent concern. Whatever the reason, it has to be discussed and explored. If the supervisee is a trainee, this may reflect a growing concern in the profession that some students are offered places when it is not appropriate to do so, as when courses are desperate to fill places in order to run. Sometimes, trainees can go a long way through the process before concerns are obvious. Bramley notes that 'the postgraduate supervisee who makes the supervisor wonder how on earth she got through the selection process for training in the first place poses particularly difficult problems' (1996: 27).

If the supervisee is in training, the contract or agreement between the supervisor and the training body should include procedures to be followed whenever there are anxieties about the standard of the work. Usually, the first step is, again, to explore the concerns with the supervisee to see if they can be effectively addressed and sufficient changes made without taking it any further. The second step often involves contacting the tutor or course director, generally with the knowledge of the student. A training course ultimately carries responsibility for deciding if the student should continue, but the supervisor should expect the course staff to take her or his concerns seriously. Failure to do so may necessitate the supervisor's contacting the institution that has the course in its programme or, if it is an accredited course, the accrediting body.

The focus of any action or response is that it is the client who is in the end the most important factor. It can be helpful for the supervisor to consult, either with her or his own supervisor or with experienced colleagues. If the concern relates to a specific piece of work, the following questions could be usefully explored with the supervisee. Is the piece of work beyond their knowledge and expertise? Is it triggering difficult and unresolved personal issues? Is the power either of the transference or of the counter-transference such that the supervisee is becoming therapeutically paralysed and therefore responding in a non-therapeutic manner? If it is a particular case, it is also worth considering if the supervisee is having sufficient supervision on it, whether the client is matched to the supervisee's experience or even if the supervisor has the necessary expertise.

Clearly, resolution from that point on depends on which, if any, of these factors are relevant. If the source of the difficulty can be discovered, various options and interventions can be considered. One of these may be to help the supervisee withdraw in an appropriate manner and over an appropriate number of sessions from that piece of work. A panic reaction that leads to rapid termination with a client is not at all desirable. A planned and monitored transition is much to be preferred. If the level of concern is not too great, there is a possibility of resolution within supervision or by consulting with an agency or a training course where that is relevant. We are considering here a very different scenario from one where there has been an obvious breach of a code of ethics. But, if the concern is too serious to resolve in supervision alone, such as helping the supervisee to extricate themselves from a particular case, clearly more definite and perhaps swifter action is necessary.

It is potentially much more complex if there is a general dissatisfaction overall with a supervisee's work. Again, this first needs to be discussed with her or him. If he or she is newly qualified or just starting out in practice, he or she may be in a situation where there is an expectation to work well beyond her or his skill level. Alternatively, supervisees may be inadequately trained, through no fault of their own, or their training may have failed to equip them for the complexity of the work that is encountered in current practice. But again, whatever the situation, poor practice cannot be ignored, and supervisors have a duty to confront the issue and explore the circumstances. If a supervisee refuses to discuss the work, or insists that there are no problems, the supervisor is in a dilemma. The supervisor could refuse to continue with the supervision, but potentially that just places the problem with someone else, who may take a while to recognize it, and in the meantime clients might be left unprotected. Supervisees may elect to vote with their feet when confronted with poor practice, especially if they can choose their supervisor. If such a stalemate occurs, and the supervisor gets nowhere in resolving the situation, the options left include contacting the supervisee's employer (where this applies), the training course or the supervisee's professional body. If the supervisee does not belong to a professional organization, this should have been ascertained by the supervisor at the contracting stage and would probably be a contraindication to accepting that person for supervision. Practitioners who are not employed by an agency or an organization, or who do not belong to a professional body, are potentially dangerous loose cannons. Unless there are exceptional circumstances (such as danger to clients or, even more unlikely, to the supervisee or the supervisor), steps to contact third parties should always be undertaken with the knowledge of the supervisee.

One possibility we have already mentioned is where the work of the supervisee has been satisfactory for some time and where there has previously not been this concern. When there is a recognizable change in the standard of practice, this may reflect stress, illness or trauma in the counsellor or therapist, who may need a break from the work and personal help. It is important to try to resolve this with the counsellor. It is possible sometimes for someone, who normally practises ethically and carefully, to be overwhelmed by internal pressures or external events, or a combination of the two, and yet not to notice that they are not working well. One of the signs of incipient burnout is pressing on regardless, striving to do a good job but in fact committing errors. In such a case, helping someone to see what is happening to them, and recognizing their needs and difficulties, can be a welcome relief. Time out is sometimes needed and the supervisor can help put this in place and can assist the supervisee to make suitable arrangements for her or his workload. This is, of course, more easily managed with a supervisee working in an agency, where the agency can take over the counsellor's workload in the event of illness. But supervisors may need to offer more assistance to independent practitioners who do not have anyone to automatically assume responsibility in this way.

These situations, particularly more extreme examples of bad practice, do not occur very often, but it would be a fortunate supervisor, or perhaps one who chose not to see the problem, who never encounters this issue. The supervisor who fails to act is ethically culpable if any harm is then caused to clients. Although it is an uncomfortable situation to face, supervisors have a duty to respond clearly and firmly.

* * *

4.2   One of my supervisees is particularly distressed at present following the death of a relative. Should I stop her seeing clients?

It is a reality of anyone's working life that at some time during it there can be disruption caused by illness, death and other personal circumstance. The extent to which such disruption implies that therapeutic work has to cease varies from person to person and from circumstance to circumstance. Counsellors and therapists, like the rest of the population, differ in how much stress they can manage. Some are more robust and resilient than others, although everyone has their own Achilles' heel. What one person can cope with may completely floor another. There is therefore no simple equation that can be universally applied, even if there is an important baseline, which every counsellor and therapist (and, indeed, every supervisor) must be safe to practice, and should stop if they are not.

There are clearly occasions when a person's distress is so great that effectively they cease to function and continuing to work is simply not a possibility. However, at other times the situation is less clear. The supervisee in this question is obviously distressed and has shared this with their supervisor. The supervisor will want to assess how contained and containable this distress is outside the supervisory relationship. If the practitioner has sufficient space in supervision that allows her or him to express their distress, and then feel contained and managed without any anxiety on the part of the supervisor, this can paradoxically enable the practitioner to work on. Supervision has provided a sufficient container for the distress and given enough reassurance that such feelings are manageable, however terrible they seem. It is always worth checking out how the supervisee is feeling and acting in other situations. Many therapists and counsellors who have practised over a lifetime will have had the experience at some point of either literally or metaphorically sobbing on the shoulders of friends, partners and supervisors and have, as a result of the comfort and reassurance they have received, been given enough strength and resilience to continue to work safely with clients. Unless it is absolutely clear that a supervisee really cannot work, the following steps are worth considering.

Taking some time off with a planned return

Someone in a crisis can feel so overwhelmed that sensible decision-making becomes problematic. One role of a supervisor at these times is to provide a model of containment, management and common sense, as well as being empathic, concerned and caring. If there has been a bereavement, taking time off is likely to be necessary as well as sensible, for a variety of reasons.

There is a funeral to attend, probably other people to support, and if the death is of someone close a variety of practical tasks to undertake, as well as dealing with the emotional demands and pressures of the situation. Because crises and losses are so often accompanied by feeling or fearing being out of control, it is useful to help the supervisee to exercise control where it can be done. This can be achieved by exploring how much time off needs to be taken, as well as deciding a return date: to do this provides a structure and a degree of predictability for both the counsellor and the clients. Although it is sometimes difficult to know how much time off will be needed, our own experience is that when such a strategy is discussed with supervisees they are usually surprisingly accurate in the assessment of their own needs. What they do need is someone else to ask the question, to discuss it with them and help them to focus on the best strategy. Distress can diminish the ability to monitor oneself, but this does not mean such reflection cannot be recovered with another's assistance.

Limiting the caseload

Time off may be necessary, and this might be followed by working with a limited caseload, but sometimes limiting the caseload is sufficient, without the need to take time off. Again, the supervisory role is to assist the counsellor or therapist to consider what caseload seems workable in the circumstances.

Another way of reducing the pressure is to defer taking new referrals for an agreed period. It may also be helpful to give active consideration to the types of work that may be wise to avoid, at least for a while, even when the counsellor feels able to take on more work again. For a recently bereaved counsellor, avoiding work with others who are presenting with bereavement issues seems preferable. This is not as straightforward as it seems, as it is not always obvious at assessment stage what the client will eventually reveal, but, where it is apparent, such cases might need to be avoided. They should then only be taken on again after consultation with the supervisor to ensure that the supervisee is ready to undertake such work. However, as loss of one kind or another is a universal theme in therapeutic work, counsellors need to be able to manage working with this broad theme, which appears in so many different guises.

Individual counsellors have different needs. There are different types of work, as well as presenting issues, that they may need to avoid for some time. Some will feel comfortable taking on short-term focused work while avoiding longer-term cases, and for others the opposite will be true. One of us has had the experience of the death of a long-term client in particularly tragic circumstances and felt unable to take on long-term work for some months, but new short-term work felt emotionally manageable. If short-term work is going to be problematic for the counsellor, the supervisory task is to help maintain the work safely until it is concluded, because by definition there will be an arranged end in sight. If long-term work is difficult, the therapist may need to consider referring existing clients on. This can be easier to manage if the work has only just begun and is still at the assessment stage. With more established clients, it is sometimes more appropriate to negotiate with the client to take time off and restart at a later date, perhaps providing some cover should the client need it.

It is important for the whole caseload to be considered. The counsellor may need time off from some clients, yet feel able to carry on with others. This will provide some space without having to stop completely. Continuing to see particular clients may even be supportive for the counsellor as well as the client, affirming the counsellor's competence and providing one part of daily life where things go on much the same as before. However, when a particular case is concluded, the space created should be kept free.

What also needs to be borne in mind by the supervisor is the client who is already dealing with loss, where there may well be an issue of trying to avoid an unexpected ending or break in the therapy if at all possible. Where it is clear that particular cases cannot continue, it is obvious that great care needs to be taken in deciding how to manage those clients and what to tell them. Again, this can be more easily done in an agency where there are other counsellors who may be able to take cases on or act as a temporary support. While not ideal, this type of intervention needs to be carefully considered, although there are instances where it is less damaging to conclude a piece of work than it is to continue.

The supervisor has therefore to have an eye for the needs of both the supervisee and the client. We recommend that, when working with therapists and counsellors in independent practice, the supervisor's role in informing clients is one of the aspects of the contract that should have been negotiated and agreed (see Question 3.3).

Extra supervision

If the supervisor has the space to do so, it is often appropriate to offer extra supervision at a point of crisis. But, as well as greater frequency, a different pattern to supervision might be considered: sometimes a counsellor can continue with a case where there is concern about stopping and pausing the work, as long as the counsellor can have some supervision time shortly before or after the session.

Offering telephone supervision, even if it is not normal practice, can be sufficient for many counsellors in this situation. Similarly, being available between supervisory sessions can be helpful because one of the counsellor's anxieties may be about adding to the distress through unpredictable situations in the work. In our experience, such an offer of availability has never been misused and has served to limit and manage distress, enabling the work with clients to continue safely and ethically.

Focused supervision

The key to working with supervisees who are experiencing distress is ongoing monitoring. Supervision is a process and not an event. Decisions can be made, but they can also be reviewed to ensure that they are still effective and appropriate. We have already suggested that it is necessary to try to identify those cases and scenarios that in the supervisee's current circumstances are potentially difficult or especially demanding. A crucial aspect of the supervisory process is to take special care to focus on these cases. Such a system of checks and balances is reassuring for the supervisee. It acts as a mechanism for actively supporting the work by helping the supervisee to hold and contain clients by being held and contained by the supervisor.

Being realistic – what is 'good enough'?

Counsellors and therapists generally set high therapeutic standards for themselves and aim to give the best to their clients. However, it is not always possible to manage this, and it is important to recognize that, although at times aiming at excellence is difficult, competence can be good enough. Bramley notes:

> Loss of confidence is not the sole prerogative of patients, neither is the right to command a willing ear or to have an almighty moan now and again. Supervisees often need reminding that no therapist can be one hundred per cent on form, all the time. Guilt about letting patients down only adds to existing stress levels and serves no useful purpose. (1996: 25–26)

Pragmatism therefore has its place. We have both had experiences in our own practice, as well as reported to us in supervision, where, even though tired, not feeling well or because of other difficulties, we have just sat relatively silently with clients and, if we are quite honest, have on occasions not been able to be wholly attentive. Nevertheless, the feedback from clients can be that such sessions are just as helpful as when we were more obviously empathic and available to them: they have not realized that anything was different. Such experiences should encourage practitioners, when they are struggling but still able to see clients, not to try too hard but to follow those golden rules of being there, 'keeping alive, keeping well, keeping awake' as Winnicott writes (1965: 166), leaving clever interventions aside.

Clients too should not be underestimated in their ability to cope, or overpathologized in concern for their welfare. One of us had the experience of returning to work after a fairly short absence following a family bereavement. The clients knew that the absence had been for family reasons. In the third session after resuming, one client commented that the therapist was looking less pale now, and that she would therefore talk about something in her history that was difficult. She added that she had decided not to say anything in the two previous sessions as she realized her therapist was not looking 'quite herself'. When the therapist tried to address this – feeling somewhat guilt stricken and concerned – the client described how she had really appreciated the work she and her therapist had done together. She went on to say that she had found it very validating that she had been given a reason for her therapist's absence, and that it had been deeply significant for her to make a decision to leave certain difficult topics until, in her perception, the therapist looked better. Her experience as a child was that there had been no containment by anyone of any problems that arose, and she was pleased that finally she had been able to act differently. She also commented that the therapist should not underestimate how important it was for her as a client to feel that on this occasion she could offer some care to her therapist.

While therefore in these situations therapists need to be fit enough to resume work, it also needs to be recognized that these situations are complex and that what is therapeutic is not always obvious or straightforward. Bramley notes that when she was working when unwell 'not one patient noticed. When I was fully recovered from both complaints not one registered the improvement in my therapeutic performance. We therapists often exaggerate our shortcomings whilst underestimating our patients' capacity to make use of us even if we are at death's door' (1996: 26).

It is important to take great care to monitor the work of anyone who is experiencing personal difficulties, but it is also necessary to hold in mind that therapists are human and subject to good days and bad days. They do not have to be perfect, and they need to learn that sometimes just being present is good enough. Grandiosity and perfectionism are not helpful traits.

Other forms of support

Neither is grandiosity helpful in overemphasizing the significance of supervision at these times. It is, of course, important; it can be immeasurably useful; it can be a lifeline directly for supervisees and indirectly for clients. While it is the professional responsibility of the supervisor to monitor with the counsellor their fitness to practise, others can help too. Therefore, it is valuable to help supervisees identify other forms of support and to make best use of these in assisting them through difficult times.

* * *

The different responses and strategies discussed above take place, we assume, in the context of a supervisory relationship that is trusting and trustworthy and where there is sufficient flexibility for the supervisor to respond to changing and demanding circumstances for the supervisee. While acknowledging the importance of boundaries and the frame in supervision (Langs, 1994), we would argue, just as Winnicott (1965) suggests, that adaptability is a vital quality in the facilitating environment, and that the frame needs to be able to change when circumstances render it no longer viable.

However, the other necessary factor is a supervisee who has sufficient insight to know when he or she is under pressure and is able to allow the supervisor to offer help and support. Supervisees who can face their difficulties, who can acknowledge them and know something of their source and who can allow others to support them are quite probably able to work through personal difficulties, even if they need to restrict their caseload and maximize their support systems. Practitioners who permit themselves to experience distress, express it appropriately and take measures to manage their work are often exceedingly capable of putting their personal difficulties to one side during their work with clients and can focus most effectively on their work. It is those who deny or repress difficulties, and are therefore inaccessible to the type of supervisory interventions outlined in this answer, who are much more worrying, since there is then a considerable risk of their difficulties being acted out with clients.

* * *

4.3 I am not sure how much I should allow a supervisee to present personal issues in supervision. I have one who is no longer in therapy. Should I recommend that he returns to therapy?

While it is clear that therapy and supervision have essentially different purposes, to attempt to completely differentiate between them is perhaps unrealistic. At the same time, it is crucial that the two activities do not become entirely merged and undifferentiated. As Henzell notes: 'On the one hand supervision and therapy may be confused, an outcome which denies they exist for separate purposes – or, on the other, are too rigidly separated, the effect of which ignores the insights a genuinely reflective method might achieve' (1997: 72).

In a similar vein, Stoltenberg and Delworth (1987: 168–169) explore the qualities of supervision that are similar to therapy, and Yalom (1975) discusses the parallels between the two processes. Woodmansey (1987) questions the value of distinguishing not only between teaching and supervision (see Question 3.5) but also between supervision and personal therapy. And Feasey comments that:

> The closeness of the two roles, however, should not blind us to the differences between them; although I have to admit there have been a number of occasions when a client in supervision had presented me with material that could have been appropriately raised in the therapy situation, the emphasis is on *could have been, not should have been.* (2002: 47, italics in the original)

If it is argued that supervision has its roots in counselling and psychotherapy, and has a key function to play within it, it is arguable that acknowledging and exploring the processes of defences, projections, transference and counter-transference must be essential and central to both. As such it is not possible to leave the supervisee's personal issues entirely out of supervision. This implies a divide between the personal and professional that is contrary to much of the theory, particularly psychodynamic theory, which is utilized in the therapy process and explored in the supervision of it. Similarly, the reflective aspects of supervision draw upon the counsellor's use and knowledge of self as part of the professional task. If counter-transference is seen as a core concept, inevitably counsellors and therapists are called upon in supervision to consider which of their experiences in therapy are related to the client's history and experiences, and which to their own.

As this question notes, not all supervisees are in therapy and, unless therapy ever becomes an ongoing requirement for practice (which is highly unlikely and, in any event, debatable in terms of desirability), this will always be the case. Yet therapists and counsellors report experiences of supervisors, telling them to take an issue to therapy, when the supervisee sees such advice as the supervisor avoiding difficulties that need addressing in supervision itself. Most instances of this that have come to our attention usually relate to either supervisees on training courses, where they are critical of the training institution, or in supervision, where they challenge the supervisor. Supervisors and training courses therefore have to take care to be self-reflective, non-defensive and open to challenge. Otherwise, they can intervene inappropriately by suggesting therapy as the resolution of difficulties or weaknesses that actually lie within themselves or their organizations. This is a clear misuse and abuse of power and invalidating to the supervisee (see also Question 2.9).

Nevertheless, there is an important question here about the degree to which personal issues have a place in supervision. As noted above, supervision and therapy have different functions, aims and purposes. In therapy, the focus is primarily on clients and the material they present, their relationships both with the therapist and with others in their world, their past and present experiences and their conflicts and their feelings. The client is the most significant person in the therapy room.

In supervision, although in one sense the focus is obviously on supervisees since it is they who are in the room and they who are exploring their work, the primary aim remains the well-being of the client (see Question 1.1). Looking after the client inevitably involves looking after the well-being of the therapist too, even though that is a secondary consideration arising from the first. Supervision (as with many relationships) can often be experienced as having therapeutic benefit, but its purpose is not therapy in itself. As we have addressed in the answer to Question 1.3 on models of supervision, supervision is understood to have different functions; however, the client is always central.

Counsellors and therapists are also human, with life concerns that can become complex and difficult to manage, and there may be times when problems and distress threaten to overwhelm them (see Question 4.2). These issues cannot always be easily shifted onto another person for resolution, and may realistically have a place in supervision, at least for a short time. The various strategies discussed in the answer to Question 4.2 are also relevant here. Therapy, as supervisors know, and supervisees should know, is not a magic answer. It is seldom available immediately (unless the supervisee is in therapy already). Even if it seems desirable, it can take time to find and arrange. In circumstances where therapy is recommended, it may be necessary, in order to enable the counsellor to practise safely, to provide some time in supervision for the supervisee to talk about personal issues within a boundary that is held by the supervisor. One example of this boundary is when a supervisee is given the opportunity to talk about what troubles them yet the focus of the supervision does not shift. The supervisor does not become the therapist. He or she does not explore the material as they would with a client. Rather the supervisor is supportive: he or she listens and acknowledges the issue, and helps the supervisee to think about what is needed to cope with the situation. The supervisor provides space for the story to be told but then shifts the focus back to the client work, looking at the possible impact on clients of the supervisee's current situation and helping the supervisee consider how best to work in the present circumstances. The supervisor manages the time available, not losing sight of the client work. Time is also important in another sense. Helping a supervisee through a crisis by offering temporary space for some personal disclosure is entirely different from supervision turning permanently into a dumping ground for personal issues.

Being available in this way, when a supervisee has personal problems, is very different from working with them on counter-transferential issues as part of the ongoing method and theoretical underpinning of supervisory work. There are differences of depth and style between personal work as part of the supervision and personal issues temporarily obscuring the main purpose of supervision. Over a period of time, the supervisor acquires considerable knowledge about supervisees. This develops as part of a trusting relationship in which the supervisee shares personal information that has been triggered by work with clients. However, the purpose of such information is not for the supervisee to work on this material but rather to reflect on it in terms of its impact on the client–counsellor relationship and the process of therapy.

Over a period of time, supervisors, too, begin to recognize particular counter-transference reactions that can be problematic to supervisees and appropriately comment on these, sometimes identifying their potential impact on a piece of work before the supervisee does. A comment such as 'That sounds similar to what you felt working when working with Client S, when you experienced her as very much like your invasive mother' is not then an invitation to the supervisee to explore her or his relationship with their mother but does encourage reflection on the relationship with the client, on the supervisee's own reaction to it and how this might be used appropriately in the work.

Equally, it can be appropriate to explore with a supervisee when and how therapy might be helpful. Supervisors can be a reliable source of information on therapists available in the area. However, this should not be an automatic response to supervisees experiencing and disclosing temporary distress. Their greatest need at that point is to be supported by the person they already know and have trusted with that disclosure, someone who has a good knowledge of them and their work. Neither should the suggestion of therapy be an immediate response to a troublesome counter-transference. However, it may be a response when it becomes clear that what the supervisee has raised is not resolvable in supervision, is likely to recur as an issue and will continue to be a block to effective working.

Nor should the recommendation of therapy be used to deny or obscure difficulties in the supervisory relationship. Therapy, however good and potentially valuable, is not a cure-all; neither is it a rubbish dump for that which cannot be coped with in supervision. On the other hand, supervision should not be allowed to become a place where there is so much ongoing concern over the supervisee that it becomes impossible to discuss their work and ensure that clients are being safely and competently worked with. If that happens, this may well be a suitable time to discuss the possibility and advisability of therapy. We are suggesting a delicate balance here, one that the supervisor has the ultimate responsibility for monitoring: a balance between providing support without becoming a therapist, between remaining a supervisor but without being too rigid in that role and between ensuring the safety of clients by recommending therapy on the one hand and recognizing on the other that this safety can sometimes be best achieved by providing a brief opportunity for supervisees to share personal issues.

* * *

4.4   I have been approached by a counsellor who works quite differently from me but who has said she has heard I am a good supervisor. Is it wise for me to take her on? And, if I do, should I hold back on presenting ideas from my own orientation?

This question in many ways parallels an earlier question (1.7) on whether it is important for a supervisee to choose a supervisor from the same theoretical orientation. As we discuss there, the level of experience, expectations and flexibility of both parties are crucial factors.

The supervisor in this question has, however, been approached by someone of a different orientation who has elected her or him on the basis of reputation. The supervisee appears to have made an informed choice. Were this not the case, it is obviously important to be open about differences and explore the implications of this for supervision. It may be more important for a supervisee to find a skilled supervisor even where there are differences in the style of working and the theory upon which it is based. In our experience, supervisees who come from a different standpoint are often seeking out new ideas and new challenges and want an input that casts another perspective on their work. They frequently are seeking a creative dialogue that facilitates their skill and knowledge development.

As we note in Question 1.7, such an arrangement is likely to be more suitable and helpful for an experienced practitioner than for someone beginning to work as a counsellor. Experienced therapists are in a better position to integrate new ideas. They come from a position where their theoretical standpoint is already well established and their clinical practice thoroughly grounded and tested. They will therefore be much more able to filter the supervisory process appropriately, sifting the ideas that are explored and the possibilities that are discussed, and taking on board what is helpful without feeling obliged to accept all the views and interventions offered. Supervising those who have a different base can be an extremely rewarding process to all concerned, as long as it is sought voluntarily and is viewed in this creative and facilitative way.

Supervisors may none the less want to ask certain questions of themselves before entering into this type of supervision arrangement. It is not suited to supervisors who are so attached to their own theoretical perspective that they are not prepared to countenance any others. Someone who feels that their school of thought – whatever it is – is intrinsically best, or superior to others, should stick to supervisees from their own approach. They are likely to be unhelpful to supervisees unless they are genuinely interested in and open to a process that may well challenge their own views and training. Supervisors who work across different modalities and theories need essentially to be flexible, open to other approaches, not believing in a single therapeutic panacea and genuinely wanting to share their own views as well as listening to others and wanting to learn from them.

One of us has had the experience of supervising therapists in pairs' supervision, where the two supervisees came from entirely different theoretical backgrounds, and each of these was different from the supervisor's. Although this arrangement was entered into with some fear and trepidation in all three parties, and initially threw up some interesting moments of incomprehension and incredulity, it was an extraordinarily rich experience for all three. The type of learning that took place could never have occurred if there had been complete congruence of training and approach; so, while it had challenging moments for each person, it was a deeply significant experience.

Although, as we have indicated, we would generally argue against novice supervisees being placed in this context, again one of us has had the experience of supervising a student in the first year of her training course, which offered a model different from our own. This situation arose from difficulties finding placements, and the student did not want to turn the placement down on the basis of different orientation. She was part of a supervision group but was the only member from her course and orientation. In this type of situation, a supervisor needs sufficient knowledge of the other approach, and to have respect for it. Perhaps surprisingly, it all worked well. Care was taken not to undermine the student's course learning, and care was taken with interventions, for example 'Coming from my perspective, I think I'd understand the material in this way, but does that make sense to you coming from yours?'. Interestingly, it was often discovered that what initially appeared as a real difference was often more to do with the language used. Where there were differences, these were acknowledged and worked with. What was crucial to the success of this arrangement was also a group that was respectful, cooperative and open to different ideas. The group related well, being very supportive of one another in their learning. Obviously, what has to be guarded against in this situation is that any split or dissent does not get projected onto the person who is apparently 'different', and it is the task of the supervisor to ensure this does not occur or to deal with it if it does.

We believe that it would be a mistake to hold back as a supervisor from presenting views arising from one's own orientation. If this were to occur, the very richness that can be so creative in this type of scenario would be squashed at the start. Intervention means sharing and not imposing ideas. Such sharing has to be undertaken much more carefully if working with a supervisee who is still at an early stage of developing and building upon their own theoretical stance. But an experienced therapist who requests supervision from someone with a different background is likely to be robust and, we might presume, to welcome new thinking. As with all other supervisory matters, the process needs to be monitored in terms of its effectiveness, and any difficulties that are encountered need to be acknowledged and worked through.

A supervisor who undertakes supervision in this way for the first time needs to be particularly aware of the need to monitor the process but also remain confident about her or his knowledge and skill. It does not help a supervisee who has deliberately chosen someone with a different range of experience to find that they are met with an exaggerated anxiety and caution about difference. In our experience, supervising someone from a different background allows a particular kind of creativity, which comes from the freedom to let go of what we think we know and to respond much more intuitively to what we are hearing.

* * *

4.5 One of my supervisees is moving away and wants to continue with me through telephone supervision. Will that be adequate? And what additional dynamics do I need to be aware of?

Our experience is that those who opt for telephone supervision often seek out a particular person, with expertise, whom they really want to work with and, as such, are extremely committed to making it work well, since the supervision adds considerably to their own knowledge and expertise. As telephone supervisors ourselves, we share this concern to take the process very seriously and give of our best. But there are differences between telephone supervision and face-to-face supervision that need to be considered if this method is adopted. One obvious difference is the inability to see the other person (unless those participating are using technology that enables this). Therefore, nuances of body language and expression cannot easily be gauged. Of course, this is similarly the case for therapists and counsellors who have visual impairments and does not in itself render the process either invalid or inferior.

It can be hard in telephone supervision to gauge the meaning of silences, hesitations and pauses. Without seeing the person, it is harder to recognize if they are thinking, if they are upset or angry or, indeed, if they have been cut off. While this appears potentially problematic, in our experience of offering telephone supervision it has been interesting and educative to note that the relationship develops, as it does in face-to-face supervision, so that both parties become attuned to one another and able to recognize without visual signs the subtleties of the experience for the other. There is an increasing sensitization to different tones of the voice, for example where speech becomes flat or animated, or there are subtle changes in pace, in the choice of words, in the occasional stumbling over words, difficulty in finding the right phrase, or the slight sigh or variation in the pitch of the voice. Of course, this can be valuable in broader therapeutic terms as it encourages a greater awareness in the therapist, who must carefully listen to how feelings and content are expressed and to the subtleties and slight variations in speech, sound and modulation, all of which can be very significant but easily missed when body language is clearly there to observe.

In terms of its adequacy, telephone supervision can be a very good and positive choice for many people. It allows a greater range of choice of supervisor as it opens up a potentially unlimited geographical area. This is particularly important for counsellors and therapists working in rural areas where the choice of supervisors locally may be very limited, or where role overlap can be considerable. It can also match the needs of highly experienced practitioners who may have difficulty finding someone locally who has the degree of expertise and experience they are looking for, or for those working in a highly specialized field wanting a supervisor who has considerable and appropriate specialized knowledge. For example, one of us has undertaken telephone supervision and consultation in the field of working with survivors of abuse, in particular in relation to dissociation. On occasion, this has been with people at the other end of the country, either as an agreed addition to their usual supervision arrangements or as their sole supervisory input. It is also very helpful for counsellors with physical disabilities who may have considerable difficulty in accessing appropriate supervision, especially if they have mobility difficulties that limit those whom they can actually reach. Telephone supervision can open up possibilities for professional growth and development that would not otherwise be available to them.

The question arises of for whom telephone supervision is most suitable and what needs to be in place to give it the greatest chance of success. We are generally reluctant to use this form of supervision with less experienced practitioners or those in training. Experience suggests that it works best, and is indeed more than adequate, for those who are used to the supervision process, are clear on what they want, know how to present their material and how they wish to use supervision, and are able to decide freely who they want to supervise them. If the supervision is of agency-based work, it is advisable for the supervisee to check that this form of supervision is acceptable to the agency.

It is extremely helpful, indeed perhaps essential, to meet face to face at the initial contracting stage and to build in and agree on occasional face-to-face meetings. This initial meeting is important for putting in place the normal supervisory agreements and arrangements, but for many people (including supervisees and supervisors) it is also significant to know what a person looks like so as to be able to visualize them when speaking to them on the phone. Such a meeting sets the scene, at least for one party in terms of geographical location, and bases the work on something more solid than a disembodied voice. We know of practitioners who use telephone supervision where distance makes meeting impossible, but, if distance does not entirely preclude meeting, we recommend such an initial session as a helpful and sensible grounding of the work to come.

Telephone supervision therefore needs very careful planning and consideration. At the start, there needs to be some exploration of how both feel about it. Does either see any contra-indications or have any anxieties about the method? Is it really what the supervisee wants? How will any difficulties in the process be resolved? There might be an agreement that a meeting can take place if difficulties occur that cannot be resolved over the phone. Agreement on the time and place of occasional meetings is also important to put in place at this stage. We have found that with experienced practitioners who live some distance away it is possible to be flexible, for instance agreeing to meet at a convenient midpoint. It is obvious that, if this is to be done, there needs to be an arrangement for an appropriate, available and confidential venue, together with agreement about who covers the cost of the supervisor's time and travel.

In face-to-face supervision, it is not difficult for a supervisee to bring material they wish the supervisor to look at and that can be handed straight back to them at the end of the session. In telephone supervision, the sharing of written or typed material has to be more carefully planned. Details that are to be posted may need editing to ensure anonymity in case it gets lost in the post. If the supervisee works with taped material, can this be sent safely in the post or should this not be attempted? Where supervisors are used to working with a written record that the supervisee presents before discussing the case, or at the start of a presentation (see Figure 3.4, p. 73), this needs to be sent or faxed in advance. A relatively straightforward solution for those who maintain anonymous computer records is to send these · electronically.

Other than these aspects, which are particular to telephone supervision, the usual needs of contracting and commitment apply. It must be undertaken in a private, confidential space with no interruptions so that both parties can give it their full attention and consideration. This is particularly important given the other distractions that can be around if it is thought that either the supervisor or supervisee is not seeing someone face to face and therefore can be interrupted.

Telephone supervision is not for everyone. It is anathema to those who have to see the person they are talking to; they find a disembodied voice extremely disconcerting and experience it overall as essentially dislocating and fragmented. They may also value the actual journey to supervision and the space this offers for reflection, as well as find the visual contact crucial. But some who imagine it will not work can be pleasantly surprised that telephone supervision is not only professionally valuable, but itself provides a personal connection.

As with any form of supervision, there is always the possibility of it not working well: if the supervisor and supervisee are not a good match, if it is not freely chosen, if it has not been carefully considered and contracted, if the supervisor is not sufficiently competent or if the supervisee is ill-prepared or undertrained. Then it is highly unlikely to succeed. But that is not to do with the method. The great advantage of this type of supervision is that it opens up a wider choice from a greater pool of skilled practitioners which would not otherwise exist.

* * *

4.6   I have never supervised pairs before, but the centre I help in needs to introduce this for counsellors who have had individual supervision for a while. Is it basically the same as one-to-one supervision?

One of the reasons for introducing pairs' supervision is that it is more economical of supervisor time – in the same way as supervision groups can be (see Question 4.7). But pairs' supervision, like group supervision, has its own dynamic and its own particular strengths. Simply to treat it as individual supervision carried out in a pair is to miss out on all the opportunities that this form of supervision can provide.

It may seem very obvious, but when a supervisor works with two supervisees together there are three people involved. It is not one-to-one supervision, with the second person in the pair simply being an onlooker.

So let us start by distinguishing three roles in this type of supervision, since this will help clarify the different parts that each person can play.

First of all, there is the supervisor, the one who holds the session together, convenes the pair and acts as a supervisor. This person does not normally present her or his own work but has the responsibility for arranging the ground rules, which may of course be worked out with the two supervisees. He or she is also responsible for maintaining the ground rules, and in addition is the person who can encourage the most to be made of the opportunities that will come from working with a pair. Needless to say, the supervisor is of course also supervising the work presented, but this is only part of her or his role.

The ground rules include the allocation of time for presenting cases, for example it may be that each supervisee takes half the time in the session or may present once every other session. One model for an hour's session that can be considered is for one supervisee to take 50 minutes for case presentation and the other 10 minutes to mention any particular issues that need more immediate attention, but donating the time to the presenter if there is nothing urgent. The next session these roles are reversed.

The second role in this threesome is that of the presenter, who will be one of the two supervisees, taking it in turns as just described. The presenter's role is familiar and needs little further description. The third role is that of the non-presenter – the supervisee who is not at that point in the session presenting a case. This is a very important and indeed pleasurable role, and the role of the non-presenter may need to be explained to both supervisees when the initial ground rules are being agreed.

So each of the three people present has a different role at different times. The supervisees not only present cases, although when they do at that point each is in the traditional supervisee role, but each also co-supervises her or his colleague so that, when in the role of the non-presenter, each supervisee acts as a second supervisor. Similarly, the supervisor has two roles – although these are not identical to the two roles of the supervisees – sharing in the actual supervision and also facilitating the couple (or, if we include the supervisor, the threesome). These dual roles, which each person in the threesome has, are all legitimate and need to be fully entered into for pairs' supervision to work well.

Supervisors particularly need to watch, especially in the early stages of the development of the threesome, that the non-presenter does not become an observer or a sleeping partner. The non-presenter has as much right to intervene, to interrupt and to put a point of view as the supervisor. Therefore the participation of the non-presenter probably needs to be encouraged at first so that the non-presenter accepts that it is important to engage in the supervision without always having to be invited to do so by the supervisor.

And here is where the threesome really comes into its own. The supervisor needs to encourage the interaction of the non-presenter and the presenter so that from time to time they work as supervisor and supervisee, with the supervisor then in the role of facilitator. The similarity to couples' counselling is obvious. If the presenter does not take up comments that the non-presenter makes, yet they seem like valuable considerations that should not be neglected, the facilitator/supervisor can both support the non-presenter's expression of a view and observe the dynamic. This dynamic may replicate the counsellor–client relationship, thus constituting a type of parallel process (see Question 2.5). Even if what the non-presenter tries to contribute does not obviously appear relevant, if the non-presenter is ignored, this does not encourage their future participation.

It is tempting for supervisees to imagine that wisdom comes only from the supervisor – or to neglect the insights of the colleague because of competitive feelings, particularly if it feels as if a game of point-scoring is in progress. Rivalry and competition can clearly be present in a threesome, with any one of the three showing or experiencing it. Feeling excluded is a concomitant reaction related to this.

The pleasure of the non-presenter's role (and this becomes apparent every time the non-presenter is encouraged to participate in this way) comes from a unique position, that even the supervisor does not have. Whereas the supervisor can spend some of the time in free-floating attention, he or she cannot afford to enjoy such reverie all the time, because as the supervisor he or she has to stay in touch with the dynamics of the session. Unlike the supervisor, the non-presenter can free associate totally (in the knowledge that the supervisor can always pull the non-presenter back into a more rational mode if necessary) and therefore can be something of a maverick, as we like to describe the role. In this way, the non-presenter has a potentially unique position in the freedom to say what they want and should be encouraged not just to make 'supervisor'-type interventions but to speak the unspeakable. For example, while it would be possible for a supervisor to talk about her or his boredom with a particular presentation, this would have to be done rather tactfully to be an effective sharing of congruence or counter-transference; it should be easier for the non-presenter to say this, knowing that he or she is permitted to be a maverick: 'I am feeling really cut off from this discussion – it's so boring.' The non-presenter's remark may be precisely what is needed to make a breakthrough with a difficult client.

Note also that there are three dialogues that can take place, each one at any time. The supervisor and presenter is the obvious one, and discussion between the presenter and the non-presenter is a second dialogue, which we have already suggested the supervisor needs to encourage. But dialogue between the supervisor and non-presenter is also valid and often provides the presenter either with space to absorb what has been discussed so far or the opportunity to step back and listen to others working on the material, which in itself may cast new light on the case.

The skills involved in facilitating the threesome have much in common with couples' counselling. The supervisor needs to monitor non-verbal communication. To whom does the presenter speak? It should not be always to the supervisor, although it often is. Eye contact needs to reflect that both the other parties are being addressed and drawn in. The supervisor can encourage this by her or his own eye contact, looking towards the non-presenter even though the presenter insists on addressing the supervisor. It is obviously also necessary, especially at first, to watch for non-verbal cues that the non-presenter wants to intervene but is holding back perhaps because he or she thinks that the supervisor should always speak first.

Similarly, as in couples' counselling, the seating can encourage the two supervisees to address each other as much as they address the supervisor. Chairs placed at the three points of an equilateral triangle therefore support this communication, emphasizing the three people having equal value in the supervisory process and promoting the three-way conversation, which we so much stress here. It is tempting, especially where there is little space, to sit the presenter and non-presenter together. But this can lead either to their engaging only with each other or more likely singly with the supervisor and not at all with each other.

The way supervisory suggestions are made also influences the freedom of communication. If a supervisor were to address the presenter, saying 'Can you help *me* understand?', this could exclude the non-presenter; whereas 'Can you help *us* understand?' is more inclusive. At the same time, the supervisor should never assume that either the presenter or particularly the non-presenter is thinking about the material in the same way as the supervisor. A supervisor might make a suggestion and ask the non-presenter what he or she makes of the suggestion but in doing so cut across the non-presenter's own thoughts. For example, it is possible to say to the presenter, '*I'm* thinking about the tall chimneys your client referred to', and then to the non-presenter, 'What is it in the material that *you* are thinking about?'. That is better than 'I'm thinking about the tall chimneys your client referred to' and then – to the non-presenter – 'What do you make of the chimneys?'. The non-presenter and the supervisor may have completely different associations and reactions, each of which can be equally valid and potentially helpful.

As in individual supervision, it is also helpful to watch both for displacement (comments from the case that may reflect the supervisory situation) and for parallel process (where the supervisory process may reflect the case). In this situation, where there are three people present, material that particularly touches upon three-people situations may be especially relevant. For example, the non-presenter may refer to the counsellor's presenting as not being able to 'get a word in' with the client, and how this appears to parallel what the client has said about not allowing a partner to get close. But the non-presenter may also be referring less obviously to not being given much opportunity to 'get a word in' in the supervision either. The non-presenter's experience may be a similar parallel process but may alternatively (or even equally) be an expression of what the non-presenter feels in the here-and-now.

Finally, there are creative ways in which a pair of supervisees can work that extend the supervisory possibilities. They can, for example, role-play part of a session, taking the role of each person in the therapeutic relationship, so trying out alternative ways of tackling a situation; or they might engage in a gestalt-type exercise, where each represents a different part of the client (or of the counsellor) or two opposing ideas or sides of an issue; or they may play out a family situation that has just been described. But, if engaging with the material in this way, it is important that the supervisor ensures that both participants actually want to take part in such a way, that the supervisor clearly sets out the ground rules for the exercise or role-play (for example, 'We'll do this for up to ten minutes, and then stop it and unpack it'), and that the supervisor ensures there is ample time for debriefing. It is often the debriefing that reveals as much as the actual exercise. We suggest also that the presenter is able to say which role or part he or she wishes to take so that the initiative in the presentation stays with the presenter.

An alternative way of using the pair creatively, which we have seen adopted by some pairs on their own initiative, is for the non-presenter to make notes on salient points arising in the discussion to give to the presenter afterwards and so save the presenter's having to write down helpful ideas. The danger here is that the non-presenter might be confined to the role of minutes' secretary and therefore becomes less participatory in what is a truly dynamic process.

Working with a pair therefore presents exciting opportunities, which many supervisors have not recognized, imagining that they have to work in the same way as in one-to-one supervision but with an extra person present. Using the pair in the ways we have described can be even richer than one-to-one work.

* * *

4.7 Group supervision seems to me to be no more than individual supervision in a group: one person presents but just to more people than the supervisor. I sometimes feel it gets rather tedious. How can I make more use of the group setting?

As we describe in Question 4.6 on pairs' supervision, group supervision is sometimes put in place, especially by an agency or a training course, because it is economical in the use of supervisors. Where there is a limited number of experienced supervisors, or the costs of supervision become prohibitive, putting several trainees or counsellors into a group seems one way of resolving the difficulty.

Our own opinion is that group supervision has merits that are unique, and that it is therefore different from pairs' and one-to-one supervision in what it can and cannot do. We have used groups with great success, sometimes as an adjunct to individual supervision (especially with trainees) and sometimes as the sole place of supervision for counsellors and therapists.

At the outset, we need to make it clear that what we are describing is supervision in a group of counsellors who are working with individual clients. It is axiomatic that those who work as group therapists should ideally be supervised in a group, where there can be a replication of the dynamics of groups. We are not ourselves experienced group therapists and have never supervised group therapists in a group (although one of us does have experience of supervising two therapists together, who themselves conducted groups). For further information on group supervision of group therapy, see, for example, Miller (1960) and Schuman and Fulop (1989). Among useful texts on group supervision to supplement our answer we suggest Heron (1993) and Proctor (2000).

The most common form of supervision in a group, which is the one that prompts this question, is where each member of the group has a chance to present a case, which they present in the same way they would in individual supervision, and group members respond with their comments and ideas. We give this the nickname 'French cricket', since our experience of this type of presentation is that each group member addresses the person presenting, who has to field the comments in much the same way as the person with the bat in French cricket has to protect their legs from being hit by the ball! It tends to lead to a series of one-to-one conversations but in a group setting, as well as to what often feels like attack and defence. Our experience is that this type of presentation works best when the group is used to working in the many other ways we describe below, where group cohesiveness has already been generated and where members address many others in the group than just the person presenting their work.

Since there are many other ways in which a group can be used, we describe these ways to a new group, or to new members of an existing group, as set out in Figure 4.1, and we suggest that, when one member presents their work, that person chooses the method of supervision they wish the group to adopt. In a ninety-minute session, this normally allows forty-five minutes each for two presenters. We have found that a group using all these methods is best composed of between five and six members, meeting weekly. Group size is obviously relevant (see Question 3.11). Seven or eight seems to many participants to be getting too big; five plus the supervisor feels much better – and each person can present more often. Six appears to be the maximum comfortable number, although method D can accommodate more very powerfully and fruitfully.

In all the methods we describe, the interactions during and following the presentation may throw up reflections within the group of the counsellor-client interaction (as Searles demonstrates, 1965: 167–172). But of course the group may use the client material to try to deal with its own dynamics (see Question 2.5 on parallel process). For these reasons, we do not recommend group supervision unless there is a clearly designated facilitator. Usually, this will be the nominated supervisor, but in a peer group it may be one or two members, who are experienced at process observations in groups, acting for the duration of one session purely in that role and allowing the others to dwell mainly on the content of the case.

The summaries in Figure 4.1 need further explanation:

A. We have already commented upon this generally overused method. Our experience suggests that, where a group (having been excited by the other methods) tends to neglect this method, the group facilitator might need to reintroduce its relevance from time to time, to restore its validity and to show that, given the more cooperative way of working generated by other methods, it can then work well. It does allow for more material to be conveyed and for 'straight' supervision from all the other group members, but it works best when group members can engage with each other on the material as much as they do with the person presenting.

B. One person presents a case to a group for up to 15 minutes, but no one is allowed to interrupt, ask a question, etc. The other members must just listen and, if they have questions, they can talk about them in the period that follows. The presenter then listens to the group discussing the case for 20 minutes. This time the presenter must not say anything, even to correct misheard information. What matters here are the associations, questions and ideas that the other members have, which they need to address to each other, not to the presenter. Finally, the last 10

The following (and no doubt others) are possible ways of using the group:

A. Straight case presentation by one person, with everyone else responding as and when they wish.

B. Case presentation with no interruption, for no more than 15 minutes; the other group members then discuss the case for 20 minutes, with no questions to or comments from the presenter. For the last 10 minutes, the presenter engages in dialogue with the rest of the group.

C. Case presentation to sketch in the issues, followed by a role-play for 20 minutes in which the presenter plays the client and one of the members becomes the counsellor, followed by reflection on the experience from both participants and the observers.

D. Case presentation to sketch in the issues, followed by two or more members role-playing the client and significant others in the client's life, followed by reflection on the experience from participants and observers.

E. The presenter asks two members in the group to take on the role of the client and the counsellor, briefing them as necessary, and observes them at work for 20 minutes, perhaps correcting errors of fact or presentation. All then reflect on the experience: the role-players, the presenter and the observers.

F. The presenter is supervised by one other member of the group for 20 minutes, followed by reflection both on the case as well as upon the 'supervisor's' contribution.

G. Tag supervision: the presenter works in turn, but individually, with three or four members of the group, each taking the 'supervisor's' chair, followed by reflection on the case and on the process.

H. Presentation of a topic by the presenter, using case examples.

I. The presenter chooses not to present but to engage with the group in an open-agenda, free-floating discussion related to work issues.

J. The presenter chooses not to present but asks the group to review how the group itself is working.

Figure 4.1 Styles of group supervision.

minutes are free for anyone to speak – the presenter perhaps at that point addressing any questions of fact that the others had raised but, more importantly, reflecting with them on what has come out of the free-association period of 20 minutes that might be relevant to the case.

In our experience, this becomes a very popular way of using the group. It takes the person presenting out of the hot seat when it comes to feedback, allowing her or him to listen to the group free-associating to the client material. The presenter has a sense of 'being fed' in the middle part of this exercise (perhaps simply taking notes of this discussion). It is luxurious just being able to sit back and let others do the work. The group members have space to work with others, and they are not in competition with each other to the same degree as in (A) above, that is there is little competition to become the best individual supervisor to the presenter. Group dynamics clearly exist, but the presenter is not caught up in them in the same way and is left free to absorb all he or she can about the case. That certain ground has not been covered and questions remain unanswered is sometimes interesting in itself – the group's questions about what they do not know, and that which the presenter has not addressed, can be revealing. Even what appear to be mistaken lines of association can sometimes prove to be more fruitful than the presenter at first imagines.

This method needs a firm timekeeper and one who will keep the rules (usually the supervisor) – particularly not interrupting in the first period and not addressing the presenter directly in the middle period. It works well in a mixed-ability group since it gives everyone the chance to contribute without having to be at the same level – free-associating does not depend upon skill and expertise – anyone can do it! At the same time, free association in a group needs to be cultivated – those with most knowledge can intellectualize or play into a supervisory role.

The person presenting may feel at first that 15 minutes is a long time to speak. But there is no compulsion to fill that period. If he or she stops before the end of that time, there is more space for the group to work on the material, up to the last 10 minutes. But most presenters have more than enough to say and have to be stopped at the end of the allocated time.

C. Empathy is a very important quality in a therapist, and this method of supervision enables the counsellor to attempt to enter into the experience of being the client, responding to another of the group in the role of counsellor, who may or may not respond in the same way as the presenter did in the original situation. Observers can, of course, comment upon what they have thought about the work from watching both the counsellor and the client in the role-play, possibly wanting to include observations about the skills that the person playing the counsellor has shown. This is a relatively straightforward way of using the group and can also be used in pairs' supervision (see Question 4.6).

D. In this variation on the role-play method, the presenter adopts a position similar to that of the director in psychodrama, placing others into various roles that relate to the client – perhaps the client and members of the client's family (alive or dead), perhaps even different personas or aspects of the internal world of the client. We have seen this method used to great effect where the counsellor presenting asked members of the group to take on the different personas that a particular client used in relating in different settings, yet never being able to show her 'self'. We have also used this method in large-group supervision, employing the members of the supervision group as a sort of chamber orchestra of voices. When the numbers have been more than eight, we prefer to use two supervisors, one to help set up the role-play and contain it while it is running, the second to debrief all the participants as well as the presenter.

The person presenting the case asks every member of the supervision group to listen to and participate in the case history from the point of view of the character or participant in the story. It is possible, where there are enough members, for one to take on the role of the counsellor. There may be no observers, but the debriefing, which is essential in order to help group members become themselves again, can be very rich through sharing the observations and experience of the participants. This feedback includes the participants' thoughts and feelings experienced in role, but not actually expressed in the role-play itself.

The supervisor plays an important role in helping the presenter to set up and allocate the voices, always checking that a member asked to play a particular role is content to do so. It is better, once the scene has been set, for the supervisor and presenter to abstain from correcting the way people play roles, unless it is clear that the role-play is becoming too intense for any one person. Indeed, the supervisor needs to monitor the level of intensity of feeling experienced in the group, particularly if the 'voices' begin to overwhelm the person playing the client, which can happen, and which demonstrates just how much clients carry in their inner worlds.

Feedback from demonstrations of this method shows how much the presenting counsellors have learned from it about the client. Everyone feels part of the supervision exercise, and it often has a powerful effect on them as well. It may be a particularly useful tool if a counsellor is feeling stuck with a client. On the other hand, it might not be capable of being used week in and week out in a supervision group. Since it needs plenty of time for debriefing and evaluation, it may take up a double session, especially when larger numbers are used. It is more time-consuming, needing about 15–20 minutes to set up and to brief the characters, about 20 minutes to play through and as much as 45 minutes to debrief and evaluate.

One way of ending such a session is for each participant to repeat who she or he is in real life and to express one point that the counsellor might take back into the counselling.

E. This method is similar to (C) above, although here the presenter asks two other members to take the role of counsellor and client. While (C) can be used in pairs' supervision, this obviously cannot but can be used where three or more supervisees meet for supervision.

F. We have used this method in training supervisors but have also suggested it for use in regular supervision groups. The presenter chooses another member of the group to act as supervisor, and the two sit slightly apart from the group and conduct a one-to-one supervision for twenty minutes, with the others observing. For the second part of the session, the observers, as well as the two participants, comment upon the case and also upon the supervisory skills shown by the person in the role of supervisor. In supervision training as such, it is necessary to rein back discussion of the client in order to concentrate upon the supervisor's part. But, where used as part of a supervision group, both client material and supervisory skills can be discussed. This will add to the learning, and in addition this method permits group members to get some experience of being an individual supervisor; this allows the facilitator to see who may be ready to move into taking on a supervisory role.

G. Tag supervision takes its inspiration from tag wrestling, where two partners take on another pair of wrestlers, but only one from each pair is in the ring at a time. As any one of them tires, they need to reach their partner, touch hands and the partner takes their place.

Using this idea in supervision adds variety to the group, although it has to be said that some supervisees love it and others hate it as a method. The person presenting works with one other group member as an individual supervisor; the other members sit out of the presenter's sightline but are able to be seen by the person in the supervisor's chair. If the person supervising tires, or gets stuck, they can signal for one of the others to take over or, if one of those watching has a line they would wish to pursue, they signal that they wish to come and take the present supervisor's place. The two must touch hands as they pass, while the presenter carries on with the presentation. The new supervisor is likely to take them into a different aspect of the material.

The method works effectively only if those who are the supervisor, or are waiting in the wings to be the supervisor, are ready to change places. If one person clings to the supervisor role for too long it ceases to be so dynamic. As in other methods, twenty-five minutes for the tag supervision and then twenty minutes to discuss what has arisen in the supervision seems to be about the right balance.

H. The person whose turn it is to present, instead of presenting a single case, suggests a topic that may apply to a number of their own cases but is likely to apply to others' cases as well. This topic is best announced a week before the supervision group meets to enable group members to give some thought to the subject and to examples they have experience of. For example, a presenter may wish the group to discuss erotic transference, eating disorders or uncommunicative clients, always relating this to actual client material; and other members of the group can cite similar examples and strategies they have found helpful.

I. In open-agenda supervision, the presenter opts to offer the time to the whole group, for its members, including the presenter, to bring up anything related to their therapeutic work. Such a group does not start with a prepared presentation from any one member, nor does the facilitator draw up an agenda of 'who would like to discuss what'. Anyone may choose to start off with a case vignette or with any other item of concern related to their work as a counsellor or psychotherapist. What is important is that the group members take up what each person offers in terms of their own experience and casework and that the session does not concentrate upon one case or upon one person. Experience suggests that, when using this method, it is better to avoid concentrating upon one case, even though the temptation is always there to do so. Other group members need to engage through relating their own experiences.

This method can be used as a regular approach and is probably most effective when, as in a therapy group, trust in the method as well as in each other has been built up over time. But it is also a method that can be used occasionally, for example when the nominated presenter for one session is unable to be present and no one else has prepared anything to present.

An unstructured approach has its limitations, especially if one or more members are slow to come forward with case material. But this method can be used to advantage from time to time in a supervision group because it provides an opportunity to function as much as a personal support group as a supervision group. Although members may discuss cases, they may also choose to discuss other aspects of their counselling work, including the stresses they experience in their particular counselling situations. Some of these situations are likely to be reflected in the group.

As with any of the other methods, the facilitator does not join in as an ordinary member, but comments largely on the process or dynamics within the group. Although it may sometimes be valuable for the group supervisor to comment on the content of the discussion, the group membership might be presumed to have sufficient expertise to deal with the material arising about cases, etc. This enables the facilitator to concentrate upon the group process and upon keeping the group to its task. It is obviously important that both the group and facilitator are clear about the task, for example does it include counselling work only or also supervision (that is, of other counsellors by the group members)? Can other aspects of the work than casework be discussed? What are the boundaries that allow it to be a personal support group and discourage it from becoming a therapy group? There is also a danger of the facilitator making too many comments about group process and of preventing the group from working on its task by concentrating too much upon its own dynamics (this is where method (J) is more appropriate).

J. This method should be used occasionally, perhaps even being timetabled by the group supervisor, as an open-agenda group, but one that concentrates upon how the group itself is functioning. What has been said about the open-agenda group in (I) above applies as much here. But, apart from the group supervisor requesting such a review from time to time, the method may be particularly useful for any one member of the group who is not content with the dynamics of the group and can therefore use her or his allocated time to ask the group to consider its own working.

* * *

With this variety of methods, group supervision becomes a much more fruitful experience than the conventional use of the group, where one member presents a case and everyone else comments upon it. Nevertheless, as we stated at the beginning, where a group achieves the ability to play with material in this way, even the more conventional methods become richer and more useful.

* * *

4.8   How do gender, race and other such issues show themselves in supervision?

To a great extent, the degree to which issues of difference and diversity show themselves in supervision depends on the awareness of the supervisor. Supervisors, and indeed counsellors and therapists, who deny the significance and impact of culture, race, sexuality, disability, gender and class, by definition, do not perceive them as having particular significance in the process. They simply do not exist as issues. However, there are many shades of awareness. There are those who apparently benignly and sim-plistically adhere to what we would describe as a 'false equality': everyone is viewed as having equal value and is therefore treated the same. Prejudices and stereotypes belong to others and not to the supervisor or therapist in question. They are the good guys and they have sorted these issues. Others emphasize the internal world as having primary significance and thereby the external world of culture, politics and prejudice does not occupy the stage of therapy. Working solely with the unconscious and indi-vidual history neatly avoids harsh external realities and a wider historical and cultural world. Rapp (2000) describes the supervision of an apparent-ly aggressive black supervisee where:

> They uncover together the supervisee's painful experience of coming up against unthinking traces of heterosexism in the previous supervisory rela-tionship. Rigidly held and unreflected theories about genital maturity, derived from psychoanalytic writings, dating from a time when homosexual-ity was widely considered pathological, had repeatedly informed the previ-ous supervisor's approach. (2000: 95)

Many other practitioners struggle with the interface between external and internal worlds, and with the personal and the political, knowing that they work in a complex political and cultural context and also carry with them the significance of their own cultural history, both as individuals and as members of a wider community. Unless we are to become the bystanders described by Clarkson (1996), there is a responsibility actively to take note and be responsive to issues of prejudice in all its manifestations, whether in the supervisor, the supervisee, the client or others. It is crucial therefore that supervisors are aware of the different assumptions that can be made; they need to pay astute and acute attention in supervision to themselves, to their supervisees and to the context in which they are both undertaking their work. For example, some agencies work hard at ensuring their poli-cies and practice facilitate equality of opportunity for those wishing to use their service: wheelchair access, counselling at home where mobility might make access impossible, provision of counsellors who speak the range of languages used by the client group and choice of gender of counsellor are obvious examples. Others do not. A supervisor needs to be aware of what an agency's policies are, and how effectively they are carried through, when undertaking work in this context.

It is important to remember that the training most counsellors and ther-apists have received takes place against an intellectual and academic background that is based on individualism, independence and patriarchy. This has been challenged, notably by the feminist therapists (for example, Gilligan, 1982; Chodorow, 1989; Izzard and Barden, 2001) who have explored the impact of culturally determined theoretical positions on the therapeutic relationship (see also Lago and Thompson, 1996). They note that most models of therapy are Eurocentric, incorporating numerous assumptions, including the belief that only particular models of therapy work. In our view, many counselling trainings have taken more note of such challenges to traditional theories than have psychotherapy trainings, although there are some notable exceptions in the latter.

Working with diversity is a complex area, as is emphasized by much work in the field. Ffagen-Smith and Cross (1996) suggest that factors that are highly significant for one person are not so for another; for example, in one person professional identity may be more significant and carry more weight than racial identity. It is certainly important not to stereotype or to use political correctness to create other stereotypes. The following example from cross-cultural work emphasizes the complexities. One of us had the experience of two new clients on the same day: the first a young man newly arrived from Nigeria and the second a young woman from Wales. The receptionist mentioned that the person referring both clients had mentioned cultural adjustment issues but had failed to say to which client this related. The assumption was that this would be the Nigerian man. But it was not the case. His first language was English; he was much travelled, very Westernized, brought up in a diplomatic family that had travelled the world and he had settled easily. In fact, he had come to the wrong service, as he had wanted advice on a financial question and was referred on inappropriately. The young woman's first language was Welsh. She had never lived in a city before or used public transport (there was none in her region of rural Wales). She had lived on a farm and was completely overwhelmed by this transition.

While it is important that no assumptions are made about the basis of difficulties, it is also the case that to focus too much on difference can sometimes prevent the recognition of other difficulties and may, paradoxically, alienate the client. A supervisee reported how she was careful to offer a black woman client a choice of gender and culture of counsellor, but the client crossly retorted that she didn't know how many times she had to say it but she just wanted someone well trained: she didn't care about their race or gender.

We do not forget that other clients report stories of gross insensitivity to gender and culture, and other issues of difference, of not being given a choice or having their choices ignored, when the gender or some other feature in the counsellor was deeply significant to them. What is needed is attention to the individual client, to policies and practices that allow for choice (as far as this is possible), but without assuming that a client's needs can be second-guessed; they need to be assessed appropriately but not tenaciously and evangelically.

This balance between awareness and an unhelpful overawareness is a delicate one. In terms of cross-cultural supervision, Atkinson et al. (1983)

suggest that supervisors need to know about how cultural identities are formed, that they should learn about recognizing and understanding cultural norms and show willingness to explore their supervisees' anxieties around cultural differences. Lago and Thompson similarly argue that, where supervisors work with cultural diversity, it is 'professionally incumbent upon supervisors to develop their own skills in this particular area' (1996: 130).

It needs noting that whenever the word 'difference' is used there is an undercurrent of a normative stance against which human behaviour is measured. It is also worth emphasizing that issues of diversity have several layers: within counsellors and therapists, within the counsellor–client relationship; within the supervisory relationship, in relation both to clients presented and the supervisor-supervisee relationship and, encompassing all these levels, to the effects on the client, the counsellor and the supervisor of living in a society in which perceived differences are highly significant and each individual has her or his own prejudices, assumptions, stereotypes and anxieties. This pertains to sexuality, race, culture, disability, gender and so on.

These dimensions are also affected by possible bias in some of the theoretical literature that underpins the therapeutic discourse and by the fact that in many services and agencies the personnel do not reflect the population they serve in terms of age, disability and other key factors. Similarly, it is worth questioning whether there are specific cultural expectations relating to both therapy and supervision that are implicitly being assumed, when they should be more explicitly discussed.

We are therefore suggesting that awareness of difference is not only vital but also concerns a far more extensive set of differences than is often acknowledged. Perhaps it would be fair to say that supervision is full of examples of situations where difference matters. One young woman supervisee reported how her client, an elderly man in his 80s, had told her that she was such a nice young girl that he could not tell her about the concentration camps he had been in. He explained that at his age and from his background, which he described as working class, you just did not say these things to 'girls', and he would feel bad if he did. There are obvious issues here relating to age, gender and class. Another supervisee reported how she was assessing a young man who was the sole survivor of a car crash. She asked him if he would like to see a man or a woman, and he replied: 'You don't understand lads; I'd talk to me mum or me girlfriend, but not mates. I go drinking or to the footie with them. I couldn't talk to a man and I could never cry in front of a man. I'd feel stupid.' Another supervisee asked her client, a woman in her 40s, the same question and she replied that she'd like to see an older man as she thought men would be better trained and qualified and would be more senior.

Then there are comments made by supervisees themselves, reported in supervision, which show similar but less excusable bias. For example, one male therapist said of a woman client that he thought she was feeling better as she had started wearing make-up, adding that all she needed now was a boyfriend, or a female counsellor talked about an aggressive young man commenting that it was just typical male behaviour and that he would doubtless grow out of it, or a female psychotherapist who was very unsure if she could work with a lesbian client as she felt she did not understand the world she was in, nor like it very much. Prejudice and stereotyping are more frequent than is sometimes acknowledged, and it is a supervisory responsibility to recognize it, draw attention to it and explore it as an issue as much as any other part of the work.

In summary, this is an aspect of the work where there are no easy answers. Supervisors have to be alert to these complexities, recognizing that clients, supervisees and supervisors all have their own belief system, their own histories and their own cultural assumptions that are part of the monitoring of supervision. The impact of these essential parts of personal identity upon therapeutic work needs to be carefully explored, and sometimes challenged. It is clearly unhelpful to make simplistic assumptions, such as gay clients are best seen by gay therapists with a gay supervisor – an example that could be repeated in matters of race, gender, disability, etc. Not only are such ideas unrealistic but, many would argue, actually fail to acknowledge the uniqueness of each situation. Whereas awareness is essential, and choice is helpful, rigidity and divisiveness are not.

Resources

Further reading

Bramley W (1996) The Supervisory Couple in Broad-Spectrum Psychotherapy. London: Free Association Books.

Carroll M (1996) Counsellor Supervision: Theory, Skills and Practice. London: Continuum.

Carroll M, Holloway E (eds) (1998) Counselling Supervision in Context. London: Sage.

Clarkson P (ed) (1998) Supervision, Psychoanalytic and Jungian Perspectives. London: Whurr.

Driver C, Martin E, Banks M (eds) (2001) Supervising Psychotherapy: Psychoanalytic and Psychodynamic Perspectives. London: Sage.

Dryden W, Thorne B (1991) Training and Supervision for Counselling in Action. London: Sage.

Feasey D (2001) Good Practice in Supervision with Psychotherapists and Counsellors. London: Whurr.

Feltham C, Dryden W (1994) Developing Counsellor Supervision. London: Sage.

Gilbert MC, Evans K (2000) Psychotherapy Supervision: An Integrative Relational Approach to Psychotherapy Supervision. Buckingham: Open University Press

Hawkins P, Shohet R (2000) Supervision in the Helping Professions, 2nd edn. Buckingham: Open University Press.

Holloway E, Carroll M (eds) (1999) Training Counselling Supervisors: Strategies, Methods and Techniques. London: Sage.

Jacobs D, David P, Meyers D (1995) The Supervisory Encounter. London: Yale University Press.

Jacobs M (ed) (1996) In Search of Supervision. Buckingham: Open University Press.

Langs R (1994) Doing Supervision and Being Supervised. London: Karnac Books.

Lawton B, Feltham C (2000) Taking Supervision Forward: Enquiries and Trends in Counselling and Psychotherapy. London: Sage.

Shipton G (ed) (1997) Supervision of Psychotherapy and Counselling: Making a Place to Think. Buckingham: Open University Press.

Wheeler S, King D (2001) Supervising Counsellors: Issues of Responsibility. London: Sage.

References

Arlow JA (1963) The supervisory situation. Journal of the American Psychoanalytic Association 11: 576–594.

Anderson R, McLaughlin F (1963) Some observations on psychoanalytic supervision. Psychoanalytic Quarterly 32: 77–93.

Aronson S (2000) Analytic supervision. Contemporary Psychoanalysis 36: 121–132.

Atkinson D, Morton G, Sue DW (1983) Counseling American Minorities: A Cross Cultural Perspective. Dubuque, IA: Williams C. Brown.

Aveline M (1992) The use of audio and videotape-recordings of therapy sessions in the supervision and practice of dynamic psychotherapy. British Journal of Psychotherapy 8: 347–358.

BACP (undated) What is supervision? Information Sheet S2. Rugby: British Association for Counselling and Psychotherapy.

BACP (1998) How much supervision should you have? Information Sheet S1. Rugby: British Association for Counselling and Psychotherapy.

BACP (2002) Ethical Framework for Good Practice in Counselling and Psychotherapy. Rugby: British Association for Counselling and Psychotherapy.

Beiser HR (1982) Styles of supervision related to child-analysis training and the gender of the Supervisor. The Annual of Psychoanalysis 10: 57–76.

Bradley J (1997) How the patient informs the process of supervision: the patient as catalyst. In Shipton G (ed.), Supervision of Counselling and Therapy: Making a Place to Think. Buckingham: Open University Press.

Bramley W (1996) The Supervisory Couple in Broad-Spectrum Psychotherapy. London: Free Association Books.

Caligor L (1981) Parallel and reciprocal processes in psychoanalytic supervision. Contemporary Psychoanalysis 17: 1–27.

Casement P (1985) On Learning from the Patient. London: Tavistock.

Carroll M (1996) Counselling Supervision – Theory, Skills, and Practice. London: Continuum.

Casemore R (ed) (2001) Surviving Complaints Against Counsellors and Psychotherapists. Ross-on-Wye: PCCS Books.

Chodorow N (1989) Feminism and Psychoanalytic Theory. New Haven: Yale University Press.

Clarkson P (1996) The Bystander (An End to Innocence in Human Relationships). London: Whurr.

Culley S, Wright J (1997) Brief and time-limited counselling. In Palmer S (ed.), Handbook of Counselling, 2nd edn. London: Routledge.

Daniels J (2000) Whispers in the corridor and kangaroo courts: the supervisory role in mistakes and complaints. In Lawton B, Feltham C (eds.), Taking Supervision Forward. London: Sage.

Doehrman MJG (1976) Parallel processes in supervision and psychotherapy. Bulletin Menninger Clinic 40: 9–104.

Feasey D (2002) Good Practice in Supervision with Psychotherapists and Counsellors. London: Whurr.

Ffagen-Smith P, Cross WE (1996) Nigrescence and ego identity development. In Pedersen PB (ed.), Counselling Across Cultures. Thousand Oaks, CA: Sage.

Fiscalini J (1985) On supervisory parataxis and dialogue. Contemporary Psychoanalysis 21: 591–608.

Frawley O, Dea MG, Sarnat JE (2001) The Supervisory Relationship: A Contemporary Psychodynamic Approach. New York: The Guilford Press.

Frijling-Schreuder EC (1970) On individual supervision. International Journal of Psycho-Analysis 51: 363–370.

Gilbert M, Evans K (2000) Psychotherapy Supervision – An Integrative–Relational Approach. Buckingham: Open University Press.

Gilligan C (1982) In a Different Voice: Psychological theory and Women's Development. Cambridge, MA: Harvard University Press.

Griffin G (2001) Vicarious liability. Counselling and Psychotherapy Journal 4: 8–9.

Hartung B (1979) The capacity to enter latency in learning pastoral psychotherapy. Journal of Supervision and Training in Ministry 2: 46–59.

Hawthorne L (1975) Games supervisors play. Social Work (USA) May 1975: 179–183.

Heimann P (1950) On counter-transference. International Journal of Psycho-Analysis 31: 81–4.

Henzell J (1997) The image's supervision. In Shipton G (ed.), Supervision of Psychotherapy and Counselling: Making a Place to Think. Buckingham: Open University Press.

Herman JL (1992) Trauma and Recovery. New York: Basic Books/London: Pandora.

Heron J (1993) Group Facilitation: Theories and Models for Practice. London: Kogan Page.

Jacobs M (1981) Setting the record straight. Counselling 26: 10–13.

Jacobs M (1993) The use of audio-tapes in counselling. In Dryden W (ed.), Questions and Answers on Counselling in Action. London: Sage.

Jacobs M (1996a) In Search of Supervision. Buckingham: Open University Press.

Jacobs (1996b) Parallel process – confirmation and critique. Journal of Psychodynamic Counselling 2(1): 55–66.

Jacobs M (2000) Supervision of supervision? In Lawton B, Feltham C (eds.), Taking Supervision Forward. London: Sage.

Jacobs M (2004) Psychodynamic Counselling in Action, 3rd edn. London: Sage.

Jenkins P, Keter V, Stone S (2004) Psychotherapy and the Law: Questions and Answers for Counsellors and Therapists. London: Whurr.

Jenkins P (2001) Supervisory responsibility and the law. In Wheeler S, King D (eds.), Supervising Counsellors: Issues of Responsibility. London: Sage.

Jones R (1989) Supervision: a choice between equals? British Journal of Psychotherapy 54: 505–511.

Kachele H, Thoma H, Ruberg T et al. (1992) Audio-recordings of the psychoanalytic dialogue: scientific, clinical and ethical problems. In Dahl H, Kachele H, Thoma H (eds.), Psychoanalytic Process Research Strategies. Heidelberg: Springer Verlag.

Kadushin A (1968) Games people play in supervision. Social Work (USA) July 1968: 28–32.

Keiser S (1956) Panel report: The technique of supervised analysis. Journal of the American Psychoanalytic Association 4: 539–549.

Izzard S, Barden N (2001) Rethinking Gender and Therapy: the Changing Identities of Women. Buckingham: Open University Press.

Lago C, Thompson J (1996) Race, Culture and Counselling. Buckingham: Open University Press.

Langs R (1979) The Supervisory Experience. New York: Jason Aronson.

Langs R (1994) Doing Supervision and Being Supervised. London: Karnac Books.

Leonard G, Richards JB (2001) How supervisors can protect themselves from complaints and litigation. In Carroll M, Tholstrup M (eds.), Integrative Approaches to Supervision. London: Jessica Kingsley.

Levenson EA (1982). Follow the fox – an inquiry into the vicissitudes of psychoanalytic supervision. Contemporary Psychoanalysis 18: 1–15.

Lidmila A (1997) Shame, knowledge and modes of enquiry in supervision. In Shipton G (ed.), Supervision of Counselling and Therapy: Making a Place to Think. Buckingham: Open University Press.

Malan DH (1963) A Study of Brief Psychotherapy. London: Tavistock.

Mattinson J (1975) The Reflection Process in Casework Supervision. London: Tavistock.

Mearns D, Thorne B (1988) Person-Centred Counselling in Action. London: Sage.

Mearns D, Thorne B (2000) Person-Centred Therapy Today. London: Sage.

Miller S (1960) Distinctive characteristics of supervision in groupwork. Social Work 5: 1.

Mollon P (1989) Anxiety, supervision and a space for thinking: some narcissistic perils for clinical psychologists learning psychotherapy. British Journal of Medical Psychology 62: 113–122.

Mollon P (1997) Supervision as a space for thinking. In Shipton G (ed.), Supervision of Counselling and Therapy: Making a Place to Think. Buckingham: Open University Press.

Molnos A (1995) A Question of Time. London: Karnac.

Norcross JC, Halgin RP (1997) Supervision: a conceptual model. The Counseling Psychologist 10: 3–42.

Proctor B (1987) Supervision: a co-operative exercise in accountability. In Enabling and Ensuring: Supervision in Practice. Leicester: National Youth Bureau and the Council for Education and Training in Youth and Community Work.

Proctor B (2000) Group Supervision: A Guide to Creative Practice. London: Sage.

Rapp H (2000) Working with difference: culturally competent supervision. In Lawton B, Feltham C (eds.), Taking Supervision Forward. London: Sage.

Robinson V (1949) The Dynamics of Supervision under Functional Controls. Philadelphia, PA: University of Pennsylvania Press.

Rogers C (1942) Counseling and Psychotherapy. Boston, MA: Houghton Mifflin.

Ryle A (1992) Cognitive-Analytic Therapy: Active Participation in Change, A New Integration in Brief Psychotherapy. Chichester: Wiley.

Sachs DM, Shapiro SH (1976) On parallel processes in therapy and teaching. Psychoanalytic Quarterly 45: 394–415.

Schuman E, Fulop G (1989) Experiential group supervision. Group Analysis 22: 387–396.

Scott S (1998) Counselling survivors of ritual abuse. In Bear Z (ed.), Good Practice in Counselling People who have been Abused. London: Jessica Kingsley.

Searles H (1955) The informational value of the supervisor's emotional experiences. In Searles H (1965) Collected Papers on Schizophrenia and Related Subjects. London: Hogarth Press.

Searles H (1959) Oedipal love in the counter-transference. In Searles H (1965) Collected Papers on Schizophrenia and Related Subjects. London: Hogarth Press.

Searles H (1962) Problems of psycho-analytic supervision. In Searles H (1965) Collected Papers on Schizophrenia and Related Subjects. London: Hogarth Press.

Searles H (1965) Collected Papers on Schizophrenia and Related Subjects. London: Hogarth Press.

Shipton G (2000) In supervision with . . . . In Lawton B, Feltham C (eds.), Taking Supervision Forward. London: Sage.

Stoltenberg CD, Delworth U (1987) Supervising Counsellors and Therapists. San Francisco, CA: Jossey Bass.

Walker M (2003) Abuse: Questions and Answers for Counsellors and Therapists. London: Whurr.

Walker M (2004) Supervising practitioners working with survivors of childhood abuse: counter transference; secondary traumatization and terror. Journal of Psychodynamic Practice 10(2): 173–93.

Webb A (2000) What makes it difficult for the supervisee to speak? In Lawton B, Feltham C (eds.), Taking Supervision Forward. London: Sage.

Webb A, Wheeler S (1998) How honest do counsellors dare to be in the supervisory relationship?: an exploratory study. British Journal of Guidance and Counselling 26: 509–524.

Wheeler S (2000) Supervision and mature professional counsellors. In Lawton B, Feltham C (eds.), Taking Supervision Forward. London: Sage.

Winnicott DW (1964) The Child the Family and the Outside World. London: Penguin Books.

Winnicott DW (1965) The Maturational Processes and the Facilitating Environment: Studies in the Theory of Emotional Development. London: Hogarth Press.

Winnicott DW (1971) Playing and Reality. London: Tavistock.

Woodmansey AC (1987) What's wrong with psychotherapy? British Journal of Clinical and Social Psychiatry 5(3): 73–75.

Worthington EL (1987) Changes in supervision as counselors and supervisors gain experience: a review. Professional Psychology: Research and Practice 18(3): 189–208.

Yalom I (1975) The Theory and Practice of Group Psychotherapy, 2nd edn. New York: Basic Books.

Zinkin L (1988) The impossible profession. In Clinical Supervision: Issues and Techniques. London: Jungian Training Committee of the British Association of Psychotherapists.

Index

abuse 27–8, 32, 33–7, 110
accreditation 11, 12, 15, 49, 55, 83, 93
additional supervision 33–7, 68, 100–1
adjudication, professional 83
agencies 2–3, 4, 5, 21, 49, 53, 58, 60, 63, 66, 67, 68, 77, 80–1, 90, 97, 100, 111, 117, 125
agenda, setting the 90
amount of supervision 11–13, 48–9, 51, 54–5, 91–2
Anderson, R. 74–5
anti-discriminatory practice 62
anxiety 20, 39, 41, 51, 64, 69, 86–91, 98, 127
appraisal see assessment, reviews
Arlow, J. 18–19
Aronson, S. 75
assessment of clients 5, 8, 74, 99
assessment of supervisees 2–3, 9, 14, 27, 28, 62, 64, 83–7, 92
assessment of supervisors 77–80
Atkinson, D. 16–7
authority figure, supervisor as 55–8, 88
Aveline, M. 26–7

bad practice 16, 61, 80–3, 84, 85, 95–7
Banks, M. 129
Barden, N. 125
bi-polar field 3–4
behavioural therapy
    see cognitive-behavioural orientation
Beiser, H. 75
bereavement 50, 98–9
body language
    see non-verbal communication
boundaries 16, 35, 53, 103, 105

Bradley, J. 9
Bramley, W. 95, 101, 102, 129
brief therapy see short-term counselling/therapy
British Association for Counselling and Psychotherapy (BACP) 1, 2, 11, 12, 15, 22, 49, 51, 54–5, 82, 83, 93
burnout 97
bystanders 125

Caligor, L. 74
Carroll, M. 9, 74, 129
case notes 6, 29–30, 72–4, 111
Casement, P. 29
Casemore, R. 83
challenge 3, 9, 15, 17, 61, 104
change of supervisor 37, 57–8
checklist for supervisor review 78–9
child analyst supervisors 75
child protection issues 67–8
Chodorow, N. 125
choosing a supervisor 2, 13–17, 21, 37, 57–8, 87, 110, 112
Clarkson, P. 125, 129
cognitive-analytic orientation 31
cognitive-behavioural orientation 6, 8, 32
collegiality 5, 9, 10, 33, 52, 56, 69, 118
collusion 9, 37, 62
compassion 39
competencies, supervisory 59–63, 81
complaints 80–3
compliance 41
competitiveness see rivalry
confidentiality 25–6, 27, 50, 52, 68, 70
conflict 53

confrontation *see* challenge
congruence 61, 62, 114
consultation 1, 22
containment 36–7, 98, 102
content of supervision 6
contracts 4, 10, 16, 22, 23, 31–3, 35, 60, 62, 65–9, 80, 92, 93, 95, 100, 111, 112
control 47
co-operative working *see* collegiality
core conditions 8
counter-transference 6, 8, 10, 16, 34, 37, 40, 42, 43, 44, 48, 61, 62, 87–8, 96, 104105–6, 114
couples counselling 114, 115
creative techniques 6
criticism 14, 17, 38–40, 41, 55–8, 61, 62, 77–8, 89
Cross, W. 126
Culley, S. 31

Daniels, J. 83
Data Protection Act 70
David, P. 129
debriefing 116, 121
defences 6, 39, 104
definition of supervision 1–4, 10
Delworth, U. 56, 104
developmental approach 9, 10
dialectical behaviour therapy 31
didactic supervision
  see teaching in supervision
difference *see* theoretical difference; working with difference
disability 60, 66, 110, 124, 125, 128
disciplinary proceedings 82
displacement 78, 116
distance 42
Doehrmann, M. 42
Dostoevsky, F. 90
Driver, C. 129
Dryden, W. 129
dual relationships 69
duty of care 81

eating disorders 34, 50, 123
eclectic model 9, 10
educational model 9
effectiveness of peer supervision 52–4
effectiveness of supervisor 77–80

egalitarian relationship *see* collegiality
ego-ideal 88
email supervision 36
emotions 9, 40–1, 44, 47, 87, 89
empathy 8, 38, 61, 62, 120
Employee Assistance Programmes (EAPs) 32
employer 81
employment law 82
equal opportunities 60, 124–8
erotic transference 123
Ethical Framework (BACP) 24, 49, 82
ethical practice 4, 6, 22, 60, 65, 93, 96, 97
evaluation *see* assessment of trainees
Evans, K. 9, 129
extra supervision sessions 67

facilitating environment 103
fantasy 27, 43
Feasey, D. 74, 76, 104, 129
fees 65–6, 67, 111
Feltham, C. 129
feminist therapists 125–6
Ffagen-Smith, P. 126
free association 118, 120
free-floating attention 114
Fiscalini, J. 75
focus of supervision 32, 33, 101, 105
frame 36–7, 103
Frawley, O. 8
French cricket 117
frequency of supervision 12, 31, 48–9, 66, 100–1
Freud, S. 8, 42, 48
Frijling–Schreuder, E. 75
Fulop, G., 117

games supervisees play 3, 89–91
games supervisors play 3, 91
gay therapy 128
gender 60, 124–8
gestalt exercise 116
Gilbert, M. 9, 129
Gilligan, C. 125
goals of therapy 25
Griffin, G. 81
ground rules 52, 53, 113
group dynamics 60, 118, 120, 123–4
group facilitator 51, 52

group size *see* size of group
group supervision xi, 2, 6, 22, 37, 43–4,
   49–55, 60, 62, 74, 87, 92–3, 110, 112,
   117–24
group therapy 42, 43–4, 117
guilt 88, 101

Halgin, R. 9
Hartung, B. 87–8
Hawkins, P. 129
Hawthorne, L. 57, 91
Heimann, P. 42
Henzell, J. 103
Herman, J. 34
Heron, J. 53, 117
Holloway, E. 129
honesty 86–91
humanist orientation 12

insurance 68
integrative orientation xii, 9–10, 12, 21,
   60
internal supervisor 29
interpretations 41, 43, 57, 74, 78
Izzard, S. 125

Jacobs, D. 129
Jacobs, M. 26, 27, 29, 49, 93, 129
Jenkins, P. 60, 80–3
Jones, R. 3, 4, 45, 78

Kachele, H. 26
Kadushin, A. 3, 89–91
Keiser, S. 41
King, D. 129
knowledge base for supervisors 60

Lago, C. 126, 127
Langs, R. 3, 45, 46, 47, 78, 103, 129
large-group supervision 121
latency mode 87–8
Lawton, B. 129
legal issues 60, 68, 80–3, 93
Leonard, G. 81
Levenson, E. 75–6
Lidmila, A. 9
limiting caseload 99–100
line management *see* management
   supervision

living laboratory 42
long-term counselling/therapy 33, 92,
   99–100
log of supervision 70–2

McLaughlin, F. 74–5
Malan, D. 31
management supervision 1, 7, 24, 61, 82,
   98
Marriage Guidance 42
Martin, E. 129
Mattinson, J. 42, 47
maverick 114
Mearns, D. 5
mediation 83
memory 19, 26, 30, 46, 53, 92
Meyers, D. 129
Miller, S. 117
models of supervision 5, 7–11, 31, 32, 56,
   105
Mollon, P. 9, 89
Molnos, A. 31
monitoring of supervision 77–80
mutual learning xii

negative feelings, 55–8, 89
negligence 81
NHS 81, 82
non-verbal communication 78, 109, 115
Norcoss, J. 9
notes of supervision 16, 53, 63, 69–74,
   83, 92 116; *see also* case notes
number of clients 23

open-agenda supervision 123–4
open-ended therapy *see* long term
   counselling/therapy
organizations 1, 32, 50, 53, 55, 67, 68, 80–1

pairs' supervision 2, 37, 62, 110, 112–116,
   117, 120
parallel process 8, 16, 40–8, 62, 76, 115–6
peer-group supervision 36, 49–54
permission of client 27, 79
personal issues *see* supervision and
   therapy, relationship between
personal therapy 16, 75; *see also*
   supervision and therapy, relationship
   between

person-centred orientation 5
placements 85, 100
play in supervision 6, 16, 75, 76
power 56, 104
prejudice 125
primary care 31–3
private practice 85–6
process in counselling 27
process in supervision 6, 7, 51, 67–8, 123–4
Proctor, B. 7–8, 117
professional associations 4, 11, 49, 53, 55, 65, 82, 97
professional development 12
projection 6, 48, 104
psychoanalysis 11–12, 39, 42, 44, 56, 57, 74
psychodrama 121
psychodynamic orientation xii, 6, 8, 16, 27, 29, 31, 32, 44, 60, 78, 104
psychopathology 42, 60, 82, 102

qualities of supervisors 13, 62

race 60, 124–8
Rapp, H. 125
real relationship 10
recording supervision *see* notes of supervision
reflection process *see* parallel process
report writing 62; *see also* assessment
requirements of a supervisor 62–3
resistance 62
responsibility of supervisor 52, 56, 64, 68, 80–3, 84, 93, 95, 97, 125
reverie 114
reviews 7, 66, 68–9, 77, 92
Richards, J. 81
risk, clients at 67–8
rivalry 17, 39, 44–5, 64, 88, 114, 120
Robinson, V. 88–9
Rogers, C. 8
role-play 6, 51, 116, 119, 120, 121–2
roles in supervision 11
Ryle, A. 31

Sachs, D. 42
sadism 39
Schuman, E. 117

Scott, S. 36
Searles, H. 8, 29, 38–40, 41–8, 88, 89, 93, 118
self-directed learning 9
self-disclosure 61, 62
self-esteem 89
sense of humour 62
shame 88
Shapiro, S. 42
Shipton, G. 49, 93, 129
Shohet, R. 129
short term counselling/therapy 25, 31–3, 50, 60, 61, 99
size of group 50–1, 54–5, 92–3, 118
skills for supervision 60–2, 65
specialist services/supervision 33–7, 110
splitting 85
stereotypes 125, 126, 127, 128
Stoltenberg, C. 56, 104
super-ego 88
supervision and therapy, relationship between xii, 3, 8, 15–16, 50, 57, 61, 75, 90, 103–7, 124
supervision of supervision 63, 77, 93–4, 96
supervisory relationship 6, 9, 41, 44, 56, 57, 61, 103, 127
support, supervision as 3, 10, 11, 22, 53, 54, 83, 102–3, 105, 123

Taft, J. 89
tag supervision 119, 122
tape-recording xi, 8, 14, 18, 19, 26–9, 30, 59, 67, 78–80, 93, 111
teaching in supervision 8, 9, 14, 15, 62, 64, 74–7
telephone supervision 36, 37, 67, 100, 109–112
theoretical difference 16, 20–2, 65, 107–9
therapeutic relationship 6, 44
Thompson, C. 76
Thompson, J. 126, 127
Thorne, B. 5, 129
training courses (counselling/ psychotherapy) 2, 4, 5, 11, 12, 20, 21, 22, 27, 49, 51, 58, 60, 62, 67, 75, 77, 80–1, 83–7, 95, 96, 97, 104, 110, 117, 126
training in supervision xi, 13, 17, 59–63, 80, 93, 122

transactional analysis 89–91
transcripts 8, 19, 28, 30
transference 6, 10, 16, 42, 43, 45, 56, 57,
    62, 69, 87–8, 96, 104
trust 4, 8, 14, 123

UK Advocacy Network 83
UK Council for Psychotherapy (UKCP)
    11–12
unconscious communication 78
unconscious processes 8
use of supervision 5–7

verbatim 14, 17–19, 30
vicarious liability 82
visual impairment 109

Walker, M. 33, 34
Webb, A. 87
Wheeler, S. 49, 87, 93, 129
who supervision is for 1–4
Winnicott, D. 13, 75, 76, 101, 103
Woodmansey, A. 104
working with difference 124–8
working relationship 13
Worthington, E. 9
Wright, J. 31

Yalom, I. 104

Zen supervision 76
Zinkin, L. 27, 48

Printed in the United Kingdom
by Lightning Source UK Ltd.
123495UK00001B/225/A